SUFFERERS' MANIFESTO

*A Challenge to the Best in Us
and Among Us*

Owen Everard James

ABOUT THE AUTHOR

Owen Everard James is the author of **Jamaican by Birth American by Choice** and **Brackets...** *A Book of Poems*. He is a graduate of the Mico Teachers' College (now the Mico University College) in Jamaica, an honors graduate of Howard University in the United States, and a diplomate of the Institute for Advanced Technical and Vocational Training in Italy. Mr. James has lived and worked in the Caribbean, North America and East and Southern Africa. He is retired and resides in Florida.

ACKNOWLEDGEMENTS

It is surprising, the equivalence in impact of relatively minor incidents that could easily be overlooked or ignored and occurrences that, at the very outset, grab the headlines in the national press. I owe much to the impact of both for stimulating this attempt at proposing alternative approaches to understanding and addressing Jamaica's intractable problems. I recall a few incidents and occurrences that will surely put my observation in perspective.

I am asked to car sit by a friend early one Friday afternoon during one of my visits to Jamaica while he runs an errand at his busy, overcrowded bank near the docks at the Kingston waterfront. My attentiveness to my surroundings is sharp and unwavering out of concern that bad things could happen in the blink of an eye. Soon enough my focus is arrested by two small boys, barefoot, raggedly dressed but clean, pushing a homemade handcart with two recovered wooden pallets aboard. It is clear that the return of the pallets to the docks will earn them money. One is constantly pushing the cart while the other cavorts with great skill and abandon over, around and on top of the moving handcart and its cargo in between back flips on the paved roadway. They both should be in school. I wonder about their parents, the likely reasons they are not in school and the future that awaits them.

Going through departure immigration at the Norman Manley International Airport on a return trip to Florida, I cannot avert my eyes from a spellbinding, wall size Ray Chen mural of a colourful country house with rusting tin roof nestled in the bosom of a verdant hillside. The scenery tugs powerfully at my memories of the bucolic little town in which I was born. Suddenly, I realize that something appears to be out of place in the fascinating mural. There is a large, old style, off-white wall telephone jutting from the center left field of the mural. It was obviously not a part of the work of art. It is as if someone scarred the Mona Lisa by cutting out a small piece of the famous painting to accommodate a light switch on the wall against which it is hung. The impression is brutal. I later check to verify which was first in place, the telephone or the mural. The telephone was first. I wonder why no functionary had seen it fit to relocate the telephone. A small detail, perhaps, but not one without significance.

A father goes for a Saturday morning stroll with his nine-year-old son in a section of New Kingston known as the Golden Triangle. Within a block of his residence the nine-year-old is witness to the senseless murder of his father by gunmen. No one is apprehended and there is little likelihood that anyone will be. I wonder what the horrific experience will do to the nine-year-old boy, his family and the neighbors.

In principle, these seemingly unrelated incidents help to define who we are as a nation and a people. They exemplify a distressingly alarming level of dysfunction and lack of insight that make me wonder if there is any chance whatsoever of meaningful intervention that could summon some positive possibility to prevent our communal suicide. They make me wish for something; they make me want to do something; they make me want to say something. No, they really make me want to scream something. Like so many of my fellow countrymen they make me weep invisible tears and constantly wonder: what will become of our children, of our country? And so I write this Manifesto.

Then there are the people. My people. Our people. Friends, relatives, schoolmates, former professional colleagues and teachers, the surviving religious and academic institutions of my youth that are insistent reminders of how things used to be. Together, they encourage the thinking that if the memories exist, renewal and progress are better than possible. They all make for a rich, spectacular tapestry that commands my attention and demands some response to innumerable questions and concerns, some expressed, many implied or inferred. And so I write this Manifesto.

More directly, there are particular institutions and individuals that contributed to this endeavor in different ways and in varying measure. I am grateful to Dr. Pauline Knight, formerly of the Planning Institute of Jamaica (PIOJ), for her timely and useful direction to knowledgeable personnel at the PIOJ who were involved with compiling **Vision 2030 Jamaica - National Development Plan**. There is an unacknowledged, virtual institution that I now identify as the *Open University of Engaged Friends* that ceaselessly recommended or directed me to books, journals and digital sources, provided me with articles, observations and commentaries on just about every pertinent aspect of Caribbean and American history, politics and culture. Naturally, a number of excerpts from these sources are reproduced in the book.

Among the most notable of my constantly engaged friends are Bryan Mordecai, whose early observations, advice and perspective were invaluable; Dr. Basil Bryan, former Consul General of Jamaica in New York, and the quintessential Jamaican in the Diaspora, who constantly demonstrates an acute appreciation and understanding of our national dilemma; Oscar Hoo, Orville Green, Neville Powell and Lloyd Stanford, my very diligent and insightful Canadian contributors; Trevor Thomas, Leo Chambers and Hugh Hall, teachers' college classmates, keen observers, questioners of the *status quo* and responsive, encouraging sounding boards; Dr. Neville Gallimore, former Member of Parliament, Parliamentary Secretary for Foreign Affairs and on separate occasions Minister of Education and Minister of Social Security in Jamaica Labour Party administrations and his son, Andrew Gallimore, two-term Member of Parliament, former Junior Minister for Labour and Social Security. The commitment of both to Jamaica is as unquestionably certain and steadfast as is their clear concern regarding the dangers and improbability they imagine to be associated, inevitably, with the alternatives proposed in this work; Connie Burgess Hastings, whose down to earth revelations and assessments of the day to day happenings in Jamaica, especially at the interface of the ordinary Jamaican and the leadership class remain priceless; Desmond Malcolm, a genuinely concerned and committed countryman whose knowledge of, and involvement with, Jamaica's water and highway engineering problems help to advance the understanding of our broader infrastructure issues and their political implications; Guenet Gittens-Roberts, Publisher/Editor, **Caribbean American Passport**, who published an early excerpt from the book; Barry Crooks whose interest, curiosity and engagement never wavered.

My very recent and fortuitous meeting of Dr. Mildred Smith-Chang led to my introduction to her remarkable book, *The Mask Is Off*. Dr. Smith-Chang's compelling story of overcoming and capitalizing on the burdens, vulnerabilities and opportunities of illegal immigrant status in America, powerfully demonstrates the pricelessness of purpose and opportunity whether self-created or provided. At the same time, her story forcefully reveals the overwhelming potential of the multiplier effect of the Diaspora experience, however acquired, and very strongly supports my view that the Diaspora may very well represent Jamaica's trump card in the game of survival and positive progress.

Naturally, I must acknowledge the patience and gracious tolerance and understanding of my wife, Icilda, for living with the disruption inflicted by a husband who permanently occupies shared space but in a number of respects was essentially absent for protracted periods of time.

I must also thank the many naysayers to the possibilities that this effort may raise, even among those who believe it to be a pointless exercise; rather than discouraging me their points of view simply strengthened my resolve.

Finally, I must acknowledge the invaluable contribution of my friend Kenneth O'Neil Blackman to this updated edition of the book. His superlative editing skills as well as his perceptive observations have improved the overall quality of the work immeasurably.

TABLE OF CONTENTS

PART TWO | 2
MOVING AHEAD

PART THREE | 3
THE CASE FOR RADICAL CHANGE

PART FOUR | 4
THE RUBBER MEETS THE ROAD

FIRST WORDS

When I was a teenager in Jamaica there was a small group in the capital city of Kingston that self-identified as *sufferers*. They exemplified the reality that there was an underclass that was confined to the very fringes of a society in which a few were making visible, steady progress toward a better life. Such progress was seen in terms of access to education, better jobs, increasing incomes and upward social mobility.

Not too many years later, this small group of *sufferers* had so grown in numbers that the classification was widely applied and justifiably applicable across much of the nation. This had become so meaningful a term that even those of the upwardly mobile class would selectively self-identify as *sufferers* when important aspects of their progress were stymied. This was much more an attempt to better explain their current circumstances than to claim lasting membership in a class with which they conveniently identified at the time. Worthy of note is the fact that until recently there was a community just outside of Kingston called *Sufferers Heights*. The place is now known as *Windsor Heights*. Unfortunately, the dramatic change in name has yet to be matched by a comparable transformation in character and circumstances.

The plight of the *sufferers* was acknowledged to be genuine by both those who were not too far removed from the condition, and those who were so far removed, that acknowledgement was always at war with indifference. Indifference always seemed to win. Regrettably, its victory remains uninterrupted after 50 years. This reality confirms my view that we should never ever become over invested in the *status quo*; it will forever be unworthy of our permanent commitment.

Given the fact that the plight of *sufferers* was recognized as real from as early as the mid-1960s, one must wonder how and why the numbers continued to grow and metastasize like a cancer to the point where, decades later, the vast majority of Jamaicans may be accurately classified as such. It would seem that this state of affairs is the most undeniably damning evidence of all that as a nation our leaders have failed the people. This evidence forces us to question the performance and choices made by successive governments and demands that we thoroughly examine the perpetual indifference of Government as well as the amazing resignation of *sufferers* themselves to this alarming state of affairs. Could it be that in the end we are all *sufferers* to varying degrees so that, like Sisyphus, we are condemned to a condition of relentless futility?

The overriding purpose of this work is to attempt to convince a large enough number of my countrymen and fellow Caribbean islanders at home and abroad, especially some of the more influential non-political leaders and potential leaders, to pay greater attention to the trajectory of our recent history. The heading of Jamaica's ship of state is toward predictably and potentially destructive turbulence with very few signs that a timely correction is likely. Our tiller is stuck and no reliable, effective captain is anywhere to be found. There comes a time in the history of a nation when its survival demands that citizens embark on a path whose direction is more toward sacrifice than personal comfort; much less toward the ruthless accumulation of wealth by a few than toward creating opportunities for the many; much less toward the wholesale defense of the *status quo* than toward creating a vision that engenders faith in the future and minimizes the fear of change. Jamaica needs not merely to embark upon such a path but to comprehend and embrace its necessity as an imperative.

Of course, we should be deeply concerned as well at the endless and pervasive predicament of so-called Third World countries in general: *the more they change the more they remain the same* or, more accurately, in my estimation, *the more they change the worse they become.* The enchanting promise of traditional two-party-system-democracy that the lives of the faithful will improve constantly over time has never been realized. I intend to explore the fundamental reasons for this from the perspectives of Jamaican leadership in historical context, political and economic philosophy and the influence and example of the acknowledged foremost international power broker and two-party-system-democracy of the United States of America. Where useful, reference will be made to some familiar Third World countries as well.

It should not surprise that Jamaica is my singular focus in addressing the subject. Nevertheless, it is true that Jamaica's political, social and economic dilemma is illustrative of the shared dilemma in nearly all former colonized countries. Naturally, there are many ways in which to approach the task. The usual tools of research to access pertinent data apply but I am convinced that of all the available tools none can be as directly pertinent or have greater currency, urgency and insight in respect of this exercise than the personal experiences and points of view of people who continue to endure the ups and downs of life in Jamaica and other Third World countries. The pervasive nature of indiscipline at all levels of these societies, for instance, simply fuels a devastating acceptance of uncertainty and resignation in the conduct of all affairs, whether private or public.

The concerns are grave and the required response most challenging. Yet, we must dare to demand bold and timely action by our leaders in their address. Consider our forefathers, our National Heroes, and the odds they faced and addressed, sometimes posthumously. Are we willing to squander their sacrifice? In many respects our young nation has led the world, or has been at least the world's equal, in fields as diverse as exquisite foods, herbs and spices, music, athletics, cattle breeding and political foresight. It has long been accepted that Jamaica's global impact is much greater than the size of its population and land mass should warrant. Nevertheless, the leadership required at this juncture is perhaps unparalleled in our history. It is clearly crucial in its significance and critical in its timeliness on both a national and a global scale, if for no other reason than that the rest of the world continues to be in such alarming disarray at this time. Are we up to the task? Only our leaders in concert with understanding, committed, patriotic Jamaicans can answer this question. Having posed the question it is my hope that this work will help us in our approach to finding an answer.

Both history and the natural limitations of the individual citizen make it highly unlikely, if not completely impossible, that any single person may provide a blueprint for the renewal and extended future well-being of our country. Certainly, it is much more likely, realistic and perhaps more desirable that individuals of goodwill provide useful guidelines and ordered suggestions that may be supportive of this cause. National leadership as well as the ordinary citizen must effectively support and selectively utilize this amalgam on the basis of its intrinsic promise of success, simply but not solely on the basis of common sense and sheer necessity.

Lest my concern and intention be misunderstood or misinterpreted let me make clear that I do not question the motivation of the leadership class. I know too many among the group to be so inclined. Accordingly, I have no doubt that this group has the very best interest of the country at heart. Motive is never in question. Major discomfort arises at the intersection of promises, expectations and claims in regard to performance, outcomes and accountability. Good intentions are never acceptable substitutes for performance and progress. Let me add as well that no claim of unique insight or exceptional wisdom is being made in my approach to addressing our problems. However, I do claim an abiding faith in hope, even though at times this faith is very severely and much too frequently tested. What is anticipated, optimist that I am, is that those who ceaselessly love our country and have a constant interest in our welfare and our future will find it possible to set aside misleading self-interest and addictive political behavior to at least pay attention to suggested alternative approaches to resolving our intractable problems. These are the concerns that stimulate this writing.

At the start of the year the doomsday clock was set at five minutes to midnight. The clock, manipulated by atomic scientists, indicates informed estimates of how close we are as a species to extinction. Maybe as a people Jamaica should create its own facsimile as a constant reminder of our predicament as well as an incentive for the urgent engagement of leaders and citizens in the obligatory pursuit to secure our survival as a viable nation of respected and admired people. There is no doubt that there is very much to be done to address the dire straits of our circumstances. I can imagine no approach that will not seriously challenge the very best in us and among us. I suspect that there is much less time in which to act preemptively than anyone may willingly admit; yet, act we must.

The overly impatient reader may wish to go directly to part four of this volume. Even so, I implore this reader to return afterwards to the earlier sections of the book. I believe this neglect will impair the necessary understanding and appreciation of why and how as a nation we have arrived at a place that requires the unusual and in some cases radical remedies being recommended. In addition, and unfortunately, such a departure may also diminish the reader's willingness to support the view that we must address our predicament posthaste.

If the reader does not share the conviction of the necessity, power and value of a personal as well as a national vision, does not realize that we are stuck in the mud of a stultifying *status quo*, does not recognize that we have been steadily mortgaging our future at incrementally unconscionable cost, does not believe that leaders are obliged to perform and be held accountable, does not understand that the reliable future of our nation resides entirely in the hearts, minds and security of our children, then he should set this book down and read no more. If, however, he believes otherwise, I exhort him to read on in shared hope, and be moved to act in the interest of his own personal future, in the interest of all of our children as well as in the interest of a nation that has demonstrated from time to time a remarkably disproportionate ability to lead the world. Above all we dare not lose hope, for to lose hope is to reap the inevitable retribution of hopelessness.

PART ONE

DIRECTIONAL HISTORY IN BRIEF

Life teaches no lessons. Instead, with terrifying indifference it provides us with an overabundance of opportunity to learn.

1

TWO-PARTY-SYSTEM-DEMOCRACY & THE *STATUS QUO*

*S*ufferers must surely recognize their predicament. It is nevertheless a real challenge to believe that they truly comprehend its root cause. The harshest of
ironies is that the very governments that unfailingly ignore these *sufferers* and their
circumstances diligently woo them without remorse at election time. Looked at in
a somewhat less charitable way, this cultivating and harvesting of *sufferers* doubtlessly contributes directly to the organic development of areas known as garrisons
and more generally to areas accepted universally as ghettos or slums. These mer-
cilessly partisan garrisons are secure People's National Party (PNP) and Jamaica
Labor Party (JLP) enclaves in which it appears that nearly 100% of residents consistently vote the party line under the baleful eyes of enforcers who are glorified as
dons as in the movie, *The Godfather.*

These dons are power brokers and welfare providers. They determine which
members of the political party they support are elected; they play the part of
modern day Robin Hoods by paying for or subsidizing housing, food, clothing, electricity, water and school fees while protecting garrison residents from
incursions by heartlessly hostile opposition party supporters from neighboring

opposition party garrisons; they control or facilitate the trade in drugs and guns; they effectively usurp the traditional functions of government in the areas they control, including the summary application of justice up to the level of capital punishment. Not surprisingly, government contracts are among their most reliable sources of income. This illustrates a degree of politically orchestrated deference by law enforcement that is unrivalled in our history. Worse, violence in general, especially violent crime, has escalated steadily since Independence in 1962. An elaborate paper, **Urban Poverty and Violence in Jamaica**, published by Caroline Moser and Jeremy Holland in 1997 under the auspices of the World Bank Latin America and Caribbean Studies *Viewpoints* series, virtually drowns in statistical evidence making the point. Most alarming is the fact that even as crime and violence were increasing precipitously the percentage of crimes being solved by law enforcement was in decline. Remarkably, our situation has worsened since 1997.

We should be aware that there is some history regarding the direct association of politicians with known criminals. Amanda Sives' **Elections, Violence and the Democratic Process in Jamaica: 1944-2007** confirms this fact in a quotation from the front page of **The Gleaner** of November 9, 1949: *Men who should be considered to be of high dignity too often appear in the company of persons known to be of evil reputation. The election is being conducted in some quarters as if it cannot be won without the support of criminals.* Note that this is 1949. It does appear that we have had ample practice at this association to the point that we are now expert at it. Garrisons and dons exemplify the acquired expertise.

In the interim *persons known to be of evil reputation* have become dons and the de facto prime ministers of their garrisons, in addition to being recognized and accepted as genuine folk heroes in their own lifetimes. Nowhere is this made clearer than in the infamous case of the Tivoli Gardens don, Christopher Coke, a.k.a. *Dudus*, a.k.a. *President*. Evidence reveals that Coke had direct access to the very highest levels of the JLP government. For example, the government, in the person of the country's Prime Minister, intervened in the matter of his extradition by U.S. authorities. This highly questionable intervention had disastrous consequences and ultimately precipitated the untimely resignation of Prime Minister Bruce Golding in October of 2011, before he had served his full term in office.

It is strikingly relevant that the consensus among political observers is that Golding could not have been elected to his Tivoli Gardens parliamentary seat without the support of Coke. Perhaps it is even more contextually relevant and significant that Coke also thrived unhindered under the government of the PNP which governed the island for nearly two decades before the JLP came to power in 2007 under the leadership of Bruce Golding. The unavoidable conclusion must be that corruption and its agents thrive regardless of which political party is in power. Clearly, change in party does not mean change in much else. This is without doubt one of the most unforgivably flagrant assurances of the longevity and security of the *status quo*. The *status quo* lives; the nation declines; citizens pay the steepest of prices, including loss of property, their lives and the lives of their innocent children. The *status quo* is heartlessly self-serving; change is always promising of progress.

When will our political and civic leaders start to be as committed to their country in at least equivalent measure as they are committed to their own personal welfare? How long will it take these leaders to realize that if they kill the goose there will be no more golden eggs? Though currently inconclusive since cases brought against some politicians mentioned later in this text have not been settled, I will mention a few politicians and associates that have been accused and even charged with corruption in a later chapter. I readily acknowledge that "on-the-street" anecdotal evidence is certainly less reliable or acceptable than substantiated facts. Still, when these suspicions are also reflected in the press one is obliged to pay attention as well as give greater credence to these suspicions. On this basis it is not unexpected that the ordinary citizen would be highly suspicious of politicians that acquire extraordinary wealth soon after getting into office and almost unfailingly by the time they leave. Quite offensively, the bounty from their fraudulent endeavors is often shamelessly displayed.

Usually, even when there is not a scintilla of evidence that such bounty could have been acquired honorably, no retaliatory steps are taken to confiscate the questionable earnings or otherwise bring the wrongdoers to justice. In the willful absence of hard evidence the concerned citizen is left with no choice but to rely on the anecdotal alternative that is clearly the next best thing. On this account, we must bear in mind the fact that anecdotal evidence is not inevitably false. We should bear in mind as well that the denial of such evidence may only be effective if refuted by reliable evidence to the contrary. And while silence or feeble rebuttal may not signal guilt, it does strengthen the likelihood that anecdotal evidence is closer to fact than fiction.

Amazingly, there continues to be unyielding bipartisan resistance, if not open opposition and hostility, to a formalized, transparent process that would ensure the satisfactory vetting, selecting and monitoring of our politicians before elections, while in office and immediately following departure from office. This naturally gives incremental relevance, weight and singular value to the informal anecdotal alternative. In his memorable Caribbean International Network (CIN) Lecture, **"The Key to Prosperity in Jamaica,"** at the Schomburg Center, in Harlem, New York, USA, in October 2012, Douglas Orane, Chairman, GraceKennedy Limited, emphasized the point. Mr. Orane indicated that:

> The ..... issue to be addressed is the establishment of a system of integrity testing for persons who offer themselves for political office. This would require greater transparency in the selection process for candidates within each party that would satisfy the electorate of the suitability of these candidates. Also, once selected, the political representative must be held to the requirement to publicly declare their assets as required by law and prompt action taken where there are breaches.

Clearly, the primary intent here is to substantiate character and ensure the integrity of seekers of political office as well as of the process by which such office seekers are selected. The motive behind the resistance to this requirement remains suspect and should be persistently questioned. There is no doubt that available anecdotal and not so anecdotal evidence, can easily explain this highly suspect and united resistance.

It appears that our problem is twofold at its core: the one is entrenched political tribalism; the other is a complex selfishness that may be defined simply as a substantial variability in patriotism. While politics tends to be tribal, patriotism by its very nature cannot be since it is essential to a people's collective willingness to sacrifice on their county's behalf. This is especially true in times of crisis when the outcomes sought may appear distant and even unlikely from present perspective. Protracted survival in the embrace of political tribalism or inconsistent patriotism leads to a place in which indifference thrives and acquiescence grows in respect of stagnation, extensive poverty, destructive admiration of selfishness and greed, ineffective government and the wholesale failing of national institutions which are meant to serve the people and move the country forward. We should be much less concerned about party colours and much more concerned about accountability, performance and the measurement of performance on the part of those we elect to govern as well as those who lead in other areas of national life. We should all marvel as well as worry at the prolonged resignation of those among us who suffer and are marginalized. This resignation cannot be permanent and therefore has communally explosive potential.

Third World countries appear to exist in environments in which nuggets and pebbles lay side by side in the same ponds and streams of their reality. Etymologically speaking, both terms have much in common but when one has a choice in real life, it is highly unlikely that pebbles will be chosen over nuggets. It does seem that there is little or no difference in the degree of effort required in retrieving either. Yet, history tends to reveal that Third World countries more often than not choose pebbles. It is not without irony that either one in the shoe will cause discomfort. Still, one is obviously much more valuable than the other. Remarkably, we seem to discard nuggets without qualm at the earliest signs of unease.

Naturally, the circumstances provoke some distressing questions: Why do we so frequently make such poor choices? Why don't we recognize the poverty of related outcomes? Why do we remain committed to a traditional two-party-system-democracy that continues to yield results that generally fail to advance either our personal welfare or the welfare of our country? Why do we not recognize the reality that unchanged behavior in the face of unchanging problems is most unlikely to bring about changed outcomes? Why do those who suffer the most and are clearly marginalized appear so resigned to their plight? Are there opportunities to improve both our choices and the related outcomes? If such opportunities do exist, are they shrinking to the point of irrelevance as we ceaselessly recommit ourselves to the *status quo*?

Jamaica's problems are significantly and fundamentally tied to the consequences of crime, corruption, a deteriorating system of education, excessively high unemployment, especially among young people, declining regional and global competitiveness, largely questionable leadership at various critical levels in Jamaican society and Jamaica's transactional relationship with major international partners. The most notable effects include a palpably fearful and insecure society, an alarming decline in general civility, signs of severe loss of self-esteem among a disturbingly large number of Jamaican males and widespread despair, especially among a distressingly large number of citizens under the age of fifty. For reasons that should be readily obvious, the latter is a most disheartening and frightening predicament for any nation, let alone one at Jamaica's stage of development.

I am convinced that the two-party-system-democracy that has held us enthralled over all these years is incapable of effectively addressing our problems at their core in either the short or the long term. Put politely, two-party-system-democracy, as we have come to know and accept it, is proving itself to be less than capable in addressing far too many of the most intractable problems facing Jamaica as well as many other Third World countries. The system makes exploitation so easy and profitable that it almost seems to invite abuse. It also appears to be frighteningly supportive of the *status quo*. Indeed, it is proving to be less than adequate in resolving significant problems in even the most exemplary of First World, two-party-system-democracy countries - the United States of America. An excerpt from the May 2013 issue of **The Transatlantic Academy**, *The Democratic Disconnect, Citizenship and Accountability in the Transatlantic Community*, makes the point: *There is a deepening democratic disconnect between the formal government*

8

institutions of established and aspiring democracies, on one hand, and the lived democratic experience of their citizens, on the other.

For the most part, America is being run by wealthy and excessively influential special interest groups in conjunction with a minority in the Congress that purposely abuses a filibuster congressional convention to block legislation and to hold government and government programs hostage. The two-party-system-democracy allows such abuse even as the special interest groups involved vociferously claim that Democracy is under constant threat, especially now under the Presidency of Barack Obama.

While two-party-system-democracy in America does also allow for the redress of filibuster abuse, there is currently no willingness on either side of the political divide to tackle the menace. This unwillingness attests to the validity of an old Jamaican saying, *today for me, tomorrow for you*, as both political parties consider what the absence of the filibuster convention could possibly mean to their individual influence when in opposition. In essence, this harmful practice is of value to both parties although it has an unfavorable impact on the effectiveness of government and impedes the progress of the country generally. I see no fundamental difference in principle and intent between this blight and that of Jamaica's political tribalism and garrison contagion. Some Third World indiscretions are nurtured in First World countries and for identical reason – the protection of the *status quo.*

Paradoxically, however, the two-party-system-democracy does allow for radical adjustments that could save us from ourselves. On the face of it, the adjustments I will suggest may appear undemocratic to some, especially those that may consider Democracy pure and sacred. I do not believe that this is in fact the case. These adjustments can be made using the very instruments of two-party-system-democracy that continue to fail us. There can be no sacred cows as we seek solutions. This in itself presents a direct challenge to leadership at all levels of Jamaican society while encouraging us to imagine alternative routes to different and better outcomes. I am aware of the extraordinary extent of the challenge my ideas will present. In fact, I have already been told by some that the impossibility of the very first steps required to address our national dilemma – the visible setting aside of larger-than-life political egos and the two national political parties putting the welfare of country above their own – guarantees the failure of the endeavor. Still, I have already answered the question that this state of mind implies. The question is: Is there a consequence worse than personal failure? The answer is a resounding yes: the failure of an entire people as a nation state as its population descends into apathy and hopelessness.

At this pivotal point in its relatively brief history as an independent nation, Jamaica is presented with the monumental opportunity of setting an example of recovery, renewal and potential realization that would surely have regional as well as broader international impact. Such an initiative as this demands not just unusual political courage but a vision that is informed to an exceptional degree by unadulterated patriotism. I am unaware of any comparable country that has acted voluntarily on this kind of nation-transforming notion in the manner I am about to suggest.

From time to time history may record herculean yet fruitless effort. However, it more certainly and substantially recognizes, values, rewards and enshrines effort whose outcomes support individual and national progress. In truth, the state of affairs in our beloved country is as worthy of lament as it is of honest, patriotic effort to provide alternative, even novel, approaches to addressing our stubborn problems. The ideas being presented must be seen within the context of textbook history, the more recent history many of us have lived and an even larger number of us has simply endured or survived as *sufferers*. As well, the form of our future as a people should surely be of the greatest concern to every single one of us.

As a country we have been running in place, somewhat confused by the changing and often oppressive, moving landscape around us. In our confusion we frequently claim, certainly without great conviction, that we have made and are making substantial progress. At best, our progress has been and continues to be spotty and disjointed. In as much as we seem reluctant to recognize, accept and act against the causal link between politics and the stultifying scourge of spiraling crime, for example, we are creating a future that is more uncertain than it needs to be and certainly skewed more toward failure than success. We continue to fail to capitalize on the likely advantageous links among identifiable world class achievements of a relatively large number of remarkable citizens, exemplary institutions and noteworthy natural assets. Regrettably, we are an underperforming, steadily dysfunctional enterprise, unwilling to blunt selfishness and greed, seemingly unable to take the tough decisions, or to make the painful sacrifices and then objectively assess the value of outcomes against effort and cost. Performance, after all, may be no more meaningful and consequential than the measurement of its contribution.

Many Jamaicans, especially those at home, have become increasingly defensive of the *status quo* as this applies specifically to crime, productivity-robbing traffic congestion, constantly declining standards of courtesy, indifference and gross indiscipline across a wide range of activities, from road manners to the simplest of services at places of business. These are observations that some may consider unfair, callous, baseless or even unpatriotic. This could not be farther from the truth and only serves to substantiate my contention about unwarranted defensiveness. This may also indicate a persistent unwillingness to recognize a reality that the vast majority of Jamaicans at home and abroad readily acknowledge. In order to make progress we must be willing to examine the good, the bad and the ugly aspects of our circumstances. This is not only likely to be cathartic but also motivating and, most of all, instructive.

2

CLUES FROM OUR HISTORY

There are escalators and crevices in our history and dare I say in our future as well. The vast majority of these is and will be of our own making. This observation brings us face to face with questions about coincidence – conducive as well as catalytic, contextual violence, opportunity for progress beyond simple freedom, choice, consequence and responsibility on personal, institutional and national levels.

I do not intend to dwell to any significant extent on the details of our early history. Yet, in order to better reveal and understand the landscape we will explore, it is helpful that we look at some of the major occurrences in this history as these emanate from, or were directly caused by, non-traditional, independent agents such as the Maroons. There can be no doubt that these occurrences contributed directly as well as indirectly to who we are as a people and to what we are likely to become as a nation. We must appreciate that the *status quo* constantly encourages us to isolate or flee from much of this history but we certainly cannot understand it, or the predicament in which we find ourselves, by being willfully indifferent or selectively ignorant.

A number of the most transformative *status quo* threatening or defeating occurrences in our history is addressed below. I emphasize what I believe to be their most directionally relevant and influential outcomes. While arbitrarily chosen, they nevertheless support a discernible and reasonable pattern of direct relevance to significant subsequent publicly instigated and institutionally manipulated events that have eventually, and perhaps inevitably, come to overshadow many of them.

a. Coincidence – Conducive and Catalytic: 1720 – 1739

The stealthy arrival of the British in 1655 and their routing of the Spaniards from Jamaica allowed the slaves in Spanish bondage to sever themselves from their Spanish masters. These ex-slaves became independent agents known as Maroons and occupied the northern and eastern hills of Jamaica. They continuously harassed the British plantation owners and slave holders, attracted and succored significant numbers of runaway slaves through a system of *marronage*. In spite of British duplicity in the signing of peace agreements, the Maroons defeated the British in two wars during the period to secure their independence.

It is of monumental significance that a segment of the slave population was able to secure its independence from a political system that was predicated not only on the righteousness of its claim that its representatives were superior beings but its clear military ability to effectively exact a steep price for intransigence as well as effectively suppress any uprising. In Richard Dunn's **Sugar and Slavery**, the author contends that the Maroon wars were directly related to the insurrections that plagued the island during 1694 to 1704 and the number of slaves that ran away to join the Maroons. Runaways fleeing from the inevitable repression that followed these revolts joined other ex-slaves in the mountains. This activity set the stage for the Maroon Wars of 1720 to 1739. Other contributing factors included the unwarranted aggression of the planters towards the Maroons.

In retrospect, the trajectory of the Maroon Wars toward universal freedom was unstoppable. This was the nucleus of a muscular conviction among the enslaved that freedom was not merely probable but sustainable. Still, it would be a hundred years before the most substantial consequence of the Maroon Wars manifested itself in the abolishment of slavery in 1838 and an additional one hundred and twenty four years in the attainment of National Independence in 1962. Quite often we revere the mighty oak but fail to acknowledge the profound significance of the tiny acorn from which it springs.

It requires little imagination to comprehend the fitting, direct relevance and depth of meaning of the Bob Marley verse from the song, *I Shot the Sheriff*:

> *Sheriff John Brown always hated me,*
> *For what, I don't know:*
> *Every time I plant a seed,*
> *He said kill it before it grow —*
> *He said kill them before they grow.*

The Maroon Wars were the seeds that could not be killed even in hibernation. To broaden the significance of what this means we need to pay attention to the remarkable observations of both Louis Lindsay (**The Myth of Independence: Middle Class Politics and Non-Mobilization in Jamaica**) and Miziki Thame (**Reading Violence and Postcolonial Decolonization through Fanon: The Case of Jamaica**) on the place of violence or lack thereof in how we merit and value our Independence. On the one hand full-fledged violence in the form of bloody revolution against the oppressor as postulated by Martinique born political theorist Frantz Fanon is considered necessary, even vital, to guarantee the full faith and credit of any Independence. On the other, this violence is unavoidably internalized by the oppressed and turned inward upon themselves. In any event, whether by radical or graduated violence in all its forms, it is apparent that some violence is always required in the address of oppression. In this respect, even passive resistance may reasonably be seen as a form of violence on the basis of its ability to disrupt. This is especially the case from the perspective of the oppressors and their sympathizers.

Ultimately, the larger concern becomes the quality of the outcome from such violence, regardless of its type. Lindsay's contention that our Independence is basically a myth is not entirely unfounded. The truth is that at no point in our history did our leaders reject let alone destroy the subjugating linkage between our

colonial masters and ourselves. In fact, our leaders appear to have seen this continued linkage as essential for meritorious and sustainable independence. Thame's
observation that the *status quo* maintaining colonial structures of pre-Independence
were purposely kept in place as the primary means of subduing the post-colonial
population and thus further securing the *status quo,* is essentially supportive of
Lindsay's position. Together they make a highly defensible argument regarding the
substantiality of our Independence and the complicity of the leadership class. This,
of course, presents us with the quandary of whether or not the vaunted benefits of
Independence can ever be realized if the continued admiration, respect and sanctity of the *status quo* remain at the center of our political world. Does this mean
that in time even the oppressed come to embrace, not just endure, their highly cir-
cumscribed existence? May this also mean we arrive at a political equilibrium that
ensures peace but decapitates progress? We will attempt to address this complex
issue later.

To a very great extent, no reasonable assessment can avoid unsentimental
examination of the *status quo ante bellum,* literally *the state in which things were
before the war.* Basically, the Maroon Wars, for example, exemplify realized
potential as much as they obliterated the *status quo.* This is extraordinary in the
sense that the existence of such potential was not merely denied but deemed
impossible by nearly all oppressors throughout early Caribbean history. As a
result, it is understandable that they were never quite prepared for such an
unthinkable anomaly.

It may be argued, with some justification, that the abolishment of slavery is
itself an identifiable, seminal anti-*status quo* event worthy of its own individual and
superior recognition. In my opinion, however, as significant as it is in the scheme of
things, its ultimate arrival was much too dependent on conducive external forces to
warrant such credit. This does not devalue its contribution but places it in a context
that reduces the effect of the shadow it casts on the inherently unique value of what
could reasonable be considered *the first cause.* There is no event as directly contributory to abolition and our subsequent National Independence that can legitimately

eclipse the first cause nature of the Maroon Wars. It is immaterial where these may fall on the scale of associated violence mentioned earlier. What is incontestable is the iconic nature of its outcome as well as the endurance of its veneration by those whose personhood it forever substantiated and secured.

Notably, the Maroon Wars made national heroes of Nanny and Sam Sharpe. Both paid the ultimate price for their role in the Wars. Sharpe was executed by the authorities while Nanny is said to have died in battle at the hands of fellow Maroon, William Cuffee, whom today would be considered a mercenary in the pay of the planter class. A Maroon militia also existed and was often contracted by the British to assist in putting down uprisings and in the capture of runaway slaves. This militia is implicated in the apprehension of Paul Bogle, one of the principal leaders of the 1865 rebellion. While this collaboration with the British does complicate the history of the Maroons it does not denigrate the overall significance of their unique contribution to Jamaica's march to Independence.

The arrival of the British and the routing of the Spanish are conducive coincidences. They set in motion events whose major impact at the time had much more to do with the two colonial powers than with the roots of our own future as a people. In this regard, the Maroon Wars are of much greater significance. Their gravity derives much more directly from our own seizure of an unlikely opportunity than from anything else. We can legitimately claim and own every aspect of the attending consequences. These I see as truly catalytic coincidences in terms of subsequent emancipation and National Independence. This difference is not simply a matter of splitting hairs. It goes to the very heart of the contention that in terms of contribution to our survival and performance as a people and as a nation, we not only deserve more credit but must take more credit for what we have become and are becoming. True, much was inherited but even more was earned and at a price that is often devalued. At the same time we must not deny the fact that in as much as we legitimately take credit we must also accept blame where this is warranted.

b. Contextual Violence: 1865

The Morant Bay Rebellion initiates another pivotal point in our history and substantiates the earlier contention of the primacy of the Maroon Wars. It is perhaps the most graphic sprout of the entrenched effect and communal memory of the Maroon Wars and heroes Nanny and Sam Sharpe. From our vantage point its proximity of less than thirty years could make the Rebellion seem almost contemporaneous with emancipation in 1838. Its consequences appear to have been more speedily and directly commandeered by institutional entities like the colonial government represented by Governor John Eyre and his supporters and detractors in Britain. It may be argued that it was not sufficiently isolated in origin or protracted in duration to be considered for superior ranking to the Emancipation Proclamation.

Nevertheless, to my mind it is extremely difficult to deny the existential superiority that derives from being cause rather than effect. In the same manner in which the Maroon Wars instigated Emancipation and created national heroes, the Morant Bay Rebellion precipitated the dissolution of government by a Governor and an Assembly of local gentry and led to the installation of a Crown Colony regime under the direct supervision and management of the Crown in the person of a Governor and a nominated but powerless Privy Council. As in the case of the Maroon Wars, the Morant Bay Rebellion resulted in the elevation of the principals, Paul Bogle and George William Gordon, to the status of national heroes. Both were executed for the role they played in the rebellion. Less than one hundred years later Jamaica became the first English speaking colony to win Independence from Britain.

Violence appears integral to the effective transformation if not complete destruction of the *status quo*. Again I refer to the Lindsay and Thame corroboration of the place and relevance of violence in regard to national political outcomes. Hopefully, the insightful reader is now beginning to see that the construct will become even more relevant and decisive in our discussion as we approach the post-Independence years and the socio-political dilemma Jamaica now faces as a nation being torn asunder by widespread crime and violence.

We must not fail to recognize the impact of the Morant Bay Rebellion on the consciousness of the general public, especially the masses. One reliable means of observing such cultural imprinting is in the folklore and songs of the people. In this respect the lyrics of the song *96 Degrees in the Shade* from the group, *Third World*, make the point:

> *You caught me on the loose, fighting to be free,*
> *Now you show me a noose on a cotton tree,*
> *Entertainment for you, martyrdom for me...*
> *Some may suffer and some may burn,*
> *But I know that one day my people will learn,*
> *As sure as the sun shines, way up in the sky,*
> *Today I stand here a victim - the truth is I'll never die.*

The people do not forget. If they do from time to time, history enshrined in folklore, song or verse will surely remind them.

c. Opportunities for Progress Beyond Simple Freedom: 1920 – 1944

This is a period of immense opportunity for change. As we shall see, the accomplishments of the period are not independent of the previously identified and directly related events. Especially, the period reveals an accelerated readiness on the part of the masses or working class to demonstrate on their own behalf to win what they had come to understand and embrace as economic justice. We may see this realization as somewhat distant from the Maroon Wars and the Morant Bay Rebellion but we cannot see it as disconnected. It seems clear that at this juncture matters of economics are beginning to gain ascendency over matters of simple, straightforward social justice.

The transition is a necessary and timely one. It will lay the ground work for momentous change in the perception and influence of the working class at a rate that masks the strength of the obstructive forces of the *status quo*. It is also a period that appears to support very strongly the rise of leaders that are more clearly aware of and demonstrably more sensitive to the needs of the disadvantaged masses. These *new* leaders are discernibly more sophisticated and deliberate than their predecessors. They seem to recognize opportunity for leadership readily and are much more prepared to confront the *status quo* with symbiotic guile. It is unnecessary to elaborate on the biographies of members of this group that are represented here. These biographies are well known as well as easily accessible. It is of far greater importance to explore the nature of the relationship between their motivation and vision and the actions they took in their attempts to take on the *status quo* and to shape the future of a country in complex, seemingly endless transition.

d. Marcus Mosiah Garvey: Bridge Builder & Visionary

In all this, the bold, visionary activism of Jamaica's first National Hero, the Hon. Marcus Mosiah Garvey, cannot be understated or ignored. Garvey is the initial bridge between the preceding periods of natural, raw, unsophisticated but vitally necessary leadership and the clearly more sophisticated and purposely confrontational if not absolutely militant leadership in the period we are about to review. Garvey's unparalleled contribution to Black Nationalism at home and abroad is all but incomprehensible in light of its obvious improbability. As Garvey understood history and his environment, the primary instrument in achieving his goal of equality for black people was economic independence. At the time there can be no doubt that this was a most novel and radical approach. It clearly exemplifies and validates the previously mentioned departure from the intense focus on social justice to dramatic emphasis on economic liberation. In retrospect, it appears that Garvey may have been much too far ahead of his time and may have overreached in his attempts to address the economic powerlessness of his international constituency. Unfortunately, as an early archetypical visionary this was perhaps inevitable.

Garvey saw separation of the races as the only viable solution to the internationally pervasive problems of oppression and marginalization based on race. In this conviction he preached relentlessly that Europe should be for Europeans,

Asia for Asians and Africa for all black people. His amazing, epochal initiatives included the creation of the **Universal Negro Improvement Association** (UNIA). By 1919, Marcus Garvey and the UNIA had launched the Black Star Line, a shipping company that would establish trade and commerce between people of African descent in America, the Caribbean, South and Central America, Canada, and Africa. At the same time, Garvey started the **Negro Factories Association**, a series of companies whose goal was to manufacture marketable commodities in every large industrial center in the Western Hemisphere and Africa. He also set about raising an army of blacks to secure Africa for blacks and commenced the repatriation of black people to Africa. In context, by any measure, these achieve-ments can never be seen as anything less than monumental.

While Garvey was not killed in the pursuit of his vision, he was arrested for mail fraud, tried, convicted and sentenced to five years in prison in America. Understandably, the motive behind his arrest and imprisonment remains suspect. Garvey's sentence was commuted. He was released and deported to Jamaica after serving less than two years of his prison term in Atlanta, Georgia. His international reputation not only remained intact but grew as he traveled the world to spread his message of Black Nationalism, economic independence and the need for unity among all black people.

It would be excessively gracious to claim that his most audacious efforts truly succeeded in the long term. Yet, it would be equally unfair and inaccurate to say that these efforts were completely fruitless. Perhaps the most accurate conclusion is that his efforts, though implausible, were fruitful enough to stand the test of history and to continue to grow in influence internationally. Garvey bequeathed an inspiring and lasting legacy via his vision, work, speeches and writings. While there is constant controversy about the nature and extent of the contribution and relationship of Garveyism to politics and social hierarchy in Jamaica there can be no doubt that Garvey's philosophy inspired many to reconsider their selfhood. The birth and development of the now internationally recognized and generally admired indigenous Rastafarian sect and religion of Rastafari, for example, are directly linked to significant aspects of Garvey's thinking and philosophy. Garvey's *Back to Africa Movement* and purposeful self-sufficiency as an economic principle,

remain among the most steadfast driving forces behind the lasting and disproportionate influence and reputation of Rastafarians.

It is unlikely that the period under review could have been as productive or as
transformative without Garvey's extraordinary, seminal role. Especially at home in
Jamaica, it does seem that the transition from overriding concern about race based
injustice to almost strictly economic justice, marginalized the timeliness and overall influence of Garvey's contributions even as they helped substantially to direct
and advance the impact of subsequent transformative related events.

e. Alexander Bustamante & Norman Manley: The Rise of the Cousins & their Cohorts

During the period there was widespread recognition that marginalization and
exploitation of workers were common place. Publications of the period included
The Gleaner, *The Blackman*, published by Marcus Garvey, the *Jamaica Weekly*, committed entirely to the cause of workers, and the *Jamaica Standard*. They recorded
the horrendous conditions under which workers slaved after emancipation and in
which workers continued to toil in 1938, one hundred years later. Very little, if
anything at all, had changed in the interim.

Under these conditions it would not require much incentive for the impos-
ing, self-assured, opportunistic and charismatic, near white, patrician looking
Alexander Bustamante to become engaged in public debate in the press about the
rights and welfare of workers. On this account he was a prolific writer of letters to
The Gleaner and would quickly graduate from merely writing letters to the editor
to active, direct involvement with workers in their attempts to address their historic grievances. Bustamante had changed his name from William Clarke by deed
poll after returning to Jamaica in 1932 from extensive travels abroad that included
sojourns in Spain, the United States, Panama and Cuba. This name change reveals a
remarkable sensitivity to the theatrical that is not without significance. It provided
a meaningful link to an older, more stable, substantial world and doubtlessly presented a much bolder impression of the man than the name Clarke possibly could

have made at the time. Along with the obvious advantage of skin colour, it made Bustamante larger than life in a Jamaica that was only just beginning to set about defining itself. It seems that his travels as well as his exceptional political instincts adequately prepared him for the task that would become his life's work – to seek to advance the welfare of the working class constantly and decisively – even if he remained within the orbit of the colonial structures so ably explained by Lindsay and Thame.

Bustamante's cousin, Norman Washington Manley, an exceptional schoolboy athlete, veteran of the Great War, Rhodes Scholar, urbane barrister and boxing aficionado - in short, a Renaissance man - would become an able and willing partner in this endeavor. History reveals that Manley, though unquestionably brilliant, was not as instinctively shrewd or as politically prepared. He was certainly not as flamboyant or charismatic. It appears that at the very onset of the 1938 labor rebellion in Jamaica, Manley dithered briefly as to which side of the struggle he would commit his considerable legal proficiency and generally weighty influence. Not so Bustamante. He instinctively saw the need for unifying, directive leadership and did not hesitate to fill this need. Like Bustamante, Manley could not completely escape the orbit of colonial structures. Much more than Bustamante, and perhaps most likely owing to his training in British Law, Manley saw these structures as providing a necessary glide path to Independence.

We must understand that Jamaica was not unique in its circumstance or in its response. Likewise, the majority of the English speaking colonial territories in the Caribbean was in the throes of protest or rebellion. The widespread smoldering discontent among workers, discernible from the early 1930s, ignited the rebellion of 1938. One unidentified observer of the period says it best:

> *The principal causes of working class unrest and dissatisfaction were the same throughout the region: low wages; high unemployment and underemployment; arrogant racist attitudes of the colonial administrators and employers in their relations with black workers; lack of adequate or in most cases any representation; and, no established structure for the resolution*

of industrial disputes by collective bargaining. Another factor increasing
general distress and dissatisfaction regionally was the world economic crisis
which had started in the USA in 1929 and by the early 1930s was hav-
ing a residual effect internationally. The fact that the grievances caused
by these factors existed in all these colonies explains why, despite the lack
of inter-colony contacts, the labour rebellions of the 1930s were an inter-
colony phenomenon, sweeping like a wave across the region.

In Jamaica the uprisings started on the sugar plantations and spread like a wild cane field fire through Westmoreland, Trelawny, St. Mary, Clarendon and St. Thomas. In the city of Kingston workers at the waterfront and the railways along with the army of the unemployed joined in the rebellion and initiated their own industrial action. In effect, the unrest became island wide. Certainly, there were localized leaders in a number of cases, Edgar Daley in St. Mary, Robert Rumble in Clarendon and, notably, St. William Grant and A.G.S. Coombs in Kingston. Coombs' Jamaica Workers and Tradesmen Union (JWTU) was the most organized entity among the workers. However, as a countrywide endeavor the rebellion was initially uncoordinated and leaderless. It appears that Manley's response to the uprisings required deliberation; Bustamante's required no more than the opportunity itself. It is fair to say that this distinctive difference in personality would become the defining characteristic between the two stalwarts of early Jamaican politics in the search for a stable national identity.

As both men became more enmeshed in the political life of early Jamaica the more visible this difference in character variation would turn out to be. The vision and actions of both contributed considerably to the major outcomes of the period. It is very interesting and instructive to observe the dissimilarity in tenor of their responses to the *status quo* at various points in their careers. For example, Bustamante's fearless, confrontational approach to protest was literally bare breasted while Manley's was very nuanced, scholarly and doubtlessly influenced deeply by his training in the law.

Perhaps the most famous recollection of Bustamante's approach is his response to security forces that threatened to open fire at the crowd at one of his protest meetings: he is said to have bared his chest in defiance telling the police to shoot him but to leave his people alone. He was subsequently arrested and jailed along with his constant protest companion, St. William Grant. His supporters massed and demanded his release. The governor was terrified at the prospect of escalating violence. Norman Manley, concerned about this as well, successfully petitioned the governor for the release of Bustamante. In terms of the nature of current political engagement we could reasonably assume that both men were acting in concert, one as the bad cop the other as the good cop. This does not appear to have been the case, however. Their separate but connected responses to the circumstances simply exemplify the critical, lasting differences in the nature of their characters and how each may have viewed his role in the unfolding nature of Jamaican politics.

Both men eventually came to realize the importance of having working class alliances to secure their general influence and political fortunes. It was clearly not difficult to arrive at this conclusion. After all, figures of lesser light such as A. G. S. Coombs, Richard Hart, F. A. Glasspole, Frank Hill, Ken Hill and Arthur Henry demonstrated the growing influence of the labor movement. This led to the birth of the most substantial trades unions, the Trades Union Congress (TUC), the Bustamante Industrial Trade Union (BITU) and the National Workers Union (NWU). Disagreement among the founding members of the TUC and Manley led to the formation of the NWU by Manley and his supporters. Similarly, Bustamante and his supporters engulfed the fledgling JWTU union of A. G. S. Coombs to form the eponymous BITU. Both major political parties sprung from these unions. Interestingly, Bustamante was initially a member of the PNP under Manley's leadership but quickly abandoned the PNP to set up the JLP, of which he became the leader.

In spite of the commonality of the working class and unionized labor base, it is generally agreed that Bustamante's focus was predominantly working class labor centric while Manley's was access to the levers of state power. An excerpt from *Caribbean Islands: A Country Study* confirms this difference:

.... Norman W. Manley concluded as a result of the 1938 riots that the real basis for national unity in Jamaica lay in the masses. Unlike the union-oriented Bustamante, however, Manley was more interested in access to control over state power and political rights for the masses. On September 18, 1938, he inaugurated the People's National Party (PNP), which had begun as a nationalist movement supported by the mixed-race middle class and the liberal sector of the business community with leaders who were highly educated members of the upper-middle class. The 1938 riots spurred the PNP to unionize labor, although it would be several years before the PNP formed major labor unions. The party concentrated its earliest efforts on establishing a network both in urban areas and in banana-growing rural parishes, later working on building support among small farmers and in areas of bauxite mining.

It is clear that whereas Manley's approach was cautious and calibrated, Bustamante's was visceral yet nimble. Perhaps this explains why in some quarters Bustamante was seen as anti-democratic and high handed. Commentary from **The Voice of Coloured Labour, George Padmore (editor) 1945,** makes this contention, especially in regard to the fledgling Government Workers' Unions:

To counter Bustamante's anti-democratic policy and high-handed methods, two previous officials of Bustamante's union, Ken Hill and Arthur Henry, began to form unions of the Government workers early in 1942. They had left Bustamante in 1939 because he ignored individual complaints of members and because they were disgusted with the way in which he ran the union. Hill and Henry were helped in their work by Richard Hart, F. A. Glasspole and Frank Hill, all of whom had been active workers for labour since 1937. The task that these five young men took on was not an easy one. The Government workers had never been openly organized before, and when they started their unions, the Government took alarm and tried to break them up.

Notwithstanding Bustamante's apparent firm grip on the working class population, it is generally recognized that the PNP's contribution to the rapid advancement of the masses was immense. Norman Manley along with one of his most ardent early supporters, Noel N. Nethersole, is said to have *"worked voluntarily and without payment night and day for the unions, proving beyond doubt their sincere attachment to the working class of Jamaica."* Of course, it should not be overlooked that prior to the passage of laws making unions legal, a number of key figures in the labor movement was imprisoned. Noteworthy among these were Ken Hill, Frank Hill, Arthur Henry and Richard Hart who became known subsequently and famously as the **Four H's**. Obviously, both Manley and Bustamante had ample assistance as leaders of the movement towards a new Jamaica.

The nature of their individual successes and the direction in which their individual approaches to issues would take the country provide a lasting lesson in focus, survival and the clever use of presented or created opportunities. As is the case with the other distinctive agents of change, both Bustamante and Manley are in the pantheon of National Heroes.

Character differences apart, their major contributions separately and in concert provide definitive insight into a period of our history from which we may draw a number of lessons, not the least of which is that there is as much influence and power in unity as there is in difference when goals and vision are honestly aligned. Bustamante and Manley provided clear definition, structure and long-term vision for the labor movement and in so doing secured the place of the movement among the major drivers of progress for the working class. They also set the stage for a unique national identity via the adoption of the very traditional British two-party-system-democracy that was itself directly contributory to the social and economic woes that both men were obliged to confront in order to follow their vision for an inclusive and progressive society. The irony of this choice is worthy of further examination and may be more usefully explored later when we attempt to understand the shortcomings and outright failure of the system itself.

While here, however, we are left to imagine, dream and ponder, if just for a moment, what might have been had Bustamante and Manley remained together in a single political party, in support of a united political platform, pooled their considerable talents and abilities and enlarged their common vision to defy the inoculated conviction that the only way in which to move toward nationhood and self-management was via the very system that had enslaved a people and would dole out freedom as if by prescription from a flawless political pharmacopeia. Is this in principle an irretrievably lost opportunity?

f. The Matter of Choice

If you are a fatalist your interest and peace of mind may be best served by ignoring this section altogether. There are but very few things in life that we do not actively choose; our parents, when and where we are born, for example. Just about all else requires that we make a decision or allow circumstances to decide on our behalf, in which case we do choose by default. An excerpt from an earlier work, *Brackets,* expands on this contention:

> ....*not to accept the inescapability of choice renders the concept of morality moot. On this basis the entire civilized concept of crime and punishment becomes immoral and essentially meaningless.*

> *Clearly, all of our social structures, including law and religion, function on the commonly shared belief or, at a minimum, the assumption, that we choose. We choose our spouses, we choose whether or not to have children, we choose principle over expediency or vice versa, we choose our forms of government and those who govern, we choose war or peace, we choose our religion and we choose our Gods who, at times, appear to return the favor by choosing their singular representatives among us or even an entire people. And, of course, many among us sometimes choose between life and death. We choose! There are consequences!*

Choice is therefore front and center in our past, our present and our future. It is now the most crucial aspect of our political life, particularly because of the nature of our ongoing national discontent. It is indefensible to deny that every one of the national heroes mentioned made purposeful, significant choices in the pursuit of their convictions and vision. We may question the choices they made but we dare not deny the fact that they did make those choices. The entire Jamaican polity is currently faced with perhaps the most crucial set of choices in its entire history: Do we continue to genuflect to the *status quo* or do we actively, in good conscience and with clear purpose, attempt to change course in terms of how we are governed, how we hold those who govern accountable and how we transform our system of governance to meet the challenges we face in a manner equivalent to their gravity?

There can be no doubt whatsoever that we choose our political representatives and have had long practice at doing so. The great wonderment is why we repeatedly choose the same political parties and their representatives over and over again. This, in spite of the fact that over time they generally have contributed little to either resolving our numerous intractable problems or to advancing our progress in terms that are measurably positive and decisive in the lives of the vast majority of the population or the growth of the nation in total. In support of this contention let us observe briefly the evidence of our performance as a country over the past four decades. Again, I refer to the CIN address by Douglas Orane which itself appears to rely heavily on the *May 26, 2011 Document of the World Bank, Report No. 60374-JM, Jamaica Country Economic Memorandum - Unlocking Growth*. (Referred to hereafter as **World Bank Report.**) I will address sections of the latter report separately. In his commentary Orane states:

> *The Jamaican economy suffers from a chronic problem of nearly half a century of low productivity per person. We hold the world record for declining productivity over the last 40 years, whereas virtually every other country has increased productivity during the same period. We have become so accustomed to this phenomenon of low productivity that we no longer view this most critical issue as particularly important. Here are the facts:*

In 1970 the GDP per capita in constant dollars was US$3,849 per person. In 2011 it was US$3,436, a decline of just over 10% over a forty-one year period. As an industrial engineer I am deeply disturbed by this phenomenon. Even more bothersome is when we compare ourselves to other countries. For example, income per capita in Jamaica in 1960 was almost a 1/4 of that of the United States. However, by 2005 it was close to 1/8 of that of the United States. We have been falling behind instead of catching up. In contrast, we know that many developing countries which had income levels well below that of Jamaica in the 1960s are fast approaching or have joined the ranks of developed nations.

However, let me not sound like the purveyor of doom and gloom during this period in our history. There are many positives that we have achieved as a nation. Here are a few:

1. *We have pioneered the development of all-inclusive tourism in the world and we have done it through our Jamaican entrepreneurs who have flourished, and created one of the largest sectors in the Jamaican economy.*

2. *We have developed a vibrant manufacturing sector that is one of Jamaica's largest employers of our people, and simultaneously being the source of continuous innovation in products.*

3. *Our financial services sector is strong and robust, as evidenced by its ability to have successfully weathered the worldwide financial crises of the last four years.*

4. *Jamaica is one of the early adopters of cellular phone services in the developing world, with one of the highest rates of cell phone penetration and usage in the developing world.*

5. *We have created new industries that did not exist at the time of independence e.g. the Information and Communication Technology (ICT) industry that performs services in Jamaica for companies overseas, using voice and data channels.*

6. *Our music industry has been one of the most incredibly successful in the world relative to the size of our country.*

7. *More recently our sports industry has demonstrated that we are indeed world-class at carrying our young people from childhood through to the winning tape at the Olympics, groomed by our own homegrown coaches on Jamaican soil.*

In true and understandably patriotic fashion the commentary attempts to moderate the very troubling implications of generally unfavorable performance over a significant period. This may indeed offer some comfort but it cannot compensate for the depressing reality of our general circumstances over all these many years. The commentary covers forty of the fifty years since Independence. This in itself intensifies the concern that by their very nature the accomplishments noted appear to be moments or events that stand alone as individual beacons in an otherwise bleak and windy national landscape. They indicate no clear linkage to the broader need of an overarching plan and vision that Orane appears to understand so well himself. This missing link is surprising given the existence of **Vision 2030 Jamaica,** Jamaica's plan for longer term development which is mentioned by Orane and which we will discuss later. During the entire period under review Jamaica has had only JLP or PNP governments. The PNP was the governing party for eighteen consecutive years ending in 2006. Remarkably, the total time spent as the party in power since Independence is evenly split as perhaps should be the allocated praise or blame for the outcomes of the period.

In order to help us appreciate the impact of socio-political philosophy and choice we will very briefly mention the contributions of two contemporary Prime Ministers: from the JLP, Edward Phillip George Seaga, Jamaica's fifth Prime Minister, and from the PNP, Percival Noel James Patterson, Jamaica's sixth Prime Minister. Both were career politicians and spent more than a hundred years between them honing their political skills. Yet, both could not be more different in their approach to leadership at both the party level and on the national stage.

Few among us will deny the credit generally given Edward Seaga for building the financial and planning infrastructure of the country after Independence. Perhaps even fewer will question his decisive commitment and activism in respect of native arts and crafts and awareness of our national heritage. He is accurately seen as perhaps the most competent government administrator of all. An impressively large number of national institutions reveals Seaga's contribution to the development and direction of Jamaica after Independence. Significantly, these are mainly in the areas of economics and finance. They include the local banking industry in the form of the first Jamaican majority-owned commercial bank — Jamaica Citizens Bank, the nationalization of a number of banks and insurance companies and the introduction of Merchant Banking. In addition, he presided over the decimalization of the Jamaican currency and was instrumental in setting up the Jamaica Stock Exchange and the Jamaica Mortgage Bank. Not surprisingly, Seaga was seen as the preeminent financial guru at a critical juncture in our history. In short he became an institutional architect of deservedly iconic stature.

The trouble with the outcomes of most architectural endeavors, however, is that they tend to cement things in place. It is not an unfair observation that architects usually spend much of their lives designing and overseeing the building of edifices. Much of the rest of their lives is spent preserving or securing them. Seaga's legacy is not immune from this dilemma; a dilemma that must be seen as directly contributory to his bewildering refusal to accept the obvious *fait accompli* that his impressive political career had come to an end at least two election cycles sooner than he could or would accept.

There is overwhelming evidence that he was focused, decisive and unyielding, some say authoritarian and ruthless, in pursuing his goals and objectives. Traits that seem to reflect the fact of his apprenticeship under his mentor Alexander Bustamante. The most critical example of this is Tivoli Gardens, a community he created from Jamaica's first and most infamous shanty town that was appropriately known as *Back-O-Wall* or *Dungle*. Well intentioned as the establishment of a community by fiat may have been at the time, Tivoli remains the quintessential model of the garrison archetype that has come to afflict Jamaica's well-being like no other man made scourge in our history. Seaga's unwavering, compulsive support of Tivoli throughout his time in politics, whether as Prime Minister or as leader of the Opposition, is legendary and confirms his great reluctance, if not inability, to recognize and challenge one of the most injurious aspects of Jamaica's political nightmare.

This blind spot is understandable and may even be forgivable, given the nature of the community needs that Seaga saw as vital and was committed to satisfy. In part one of his two part interview with Ian Boyne on **Profile** [November 14, 2010], one of his most incisive responses went directly to the heart of the issue of political dependency in Jamaica as well as just about in all Third World countries: the unfair choice between finding solutions to issues with longer term implications versus finding solutions to the permanently immediate need for *daily bread*. This undeniable conflict between the desirable and the urgent will almost always end up in favor of the urgent. Admittedly, this is a short or even immediate term solution but in the end truly critical survival needs inevitably have far greater political traction because of their undeniable consequential potency.

It is immensely revealing to understand Seaga's view of the comprehensive nature of his care and commitment to those he believes he had rescued from hopelessness. His intent appears to have been to take care of them from the womb to the tomb. Unfortunately, as obviously attractive as such a proposition might be, the greater the likelihood of highly problematic unintended consequences. His response to a query about his authoritative style is revealing. He states that he *allowed* the members of his cabinet to dissent. Quite a telling response, I believe.

There can be no doubt that this unusual, perhaps unique, approach to social engineering at the time has left an indelible impression of Seaga as irretrievably committed to a degree of control over his constituency that, in the view of very many, was outrageously excessive and directionally dangerous. Many were concerned that his intention was to extend this degree of control to the country as a whole. Justified or not, this attributed motive is perhaps the most influential negative that leads many to question Seaga's overall stature as an exceptionally pivotal post-Independence figure. Perhaps no other choice in his entire career is more singularly instrumental in defining the legacy of Edward Seaga than his choice to maintain Tivoli as a uniquely impregnable JLP fortress. This not only isolated its residents from the surrounding communities if not from the population at large but eventually, perhaps inevitably, instigated within the residents themselves a feeling of being stigmatized and under siege. Overlooked in the Tivoli experiment is the reality that when we lock ourselves in we lock others out. Seaga was irrevocably vested in a *status quo* that he himself had diligently created with exceptional foresight and doubtlessly with the very best of intentions.

Nevertheless, as Ian Boyne states in the July 29, 2012 edition of **The Gleaner**, Seaga is still given immense credit for his political stewardship. Boyne writes:

> *None has matched that record, let alone surpassed it, since Carl Stone wrote those words in **The Sunday Gleaner** of May 2, 1992. There is no living Jamaican anywhere in the world today, as Jamaica celebrates its 50th anniversary, who has contributed as much to Jamaica as Edward Phillip George Seaga. None. When Parliament meets on Thursday for a special commemorative sitting for Jamaica 50, special honour should be given to Edward Seaga for his incalculable contribution to Jamaica - if we truly had the stomach for non-partisanship and political maturity.*

No other party or Prime Minister has spent as much continuous time in office yet accomplished comparatively so little as the PNP and Percival Patterson did from 1989 through 2006. In my estimation, this is primarily because of leadership style and political philosophy that led to a clear failure to act at a time when decisive action was warranted and necessary. It appears that Patterson was wedded to the *status quo* with such commitment that divorce or even counseling was never an option. It also appears that in this wedded zeal he subscribed to the medical caveat to first do no harm. Certainly, in what appears to be a misunderstanding of the caveat, Patterson interpreted this to mean do nothing. But there is the sin of commission as well as the sin of omission. It may be argued with much justification that the unbroken fourteen year period from 1992 to 2006 when Patterson served as Prime Minister after the resignation of his predecessor Michael Manley on account of ill health, constitutes the most unproductive and inconsequential period of government since 1962.

Still, Patterson did attend to one major infrastructure concern that has plagued the island nation for a very long time – networked highways. He should be credited with being the first Prime Minister to address this shortcoming as a matter of national priority and urgency. This was done via the now famous Highway 2000 project whose objective is to link critical areas of the country by way of more than 200 kilometers of world class highways, sections of which are tolled. It is now 2012 but the project is only about 40% complete.

It is not an unwarranted consensus that Patterson's greatest competence lay in political organization and more specifically in election planning and execution. A glance at the **Jamaica Information Service's (JIS)** *This Is Jamaica* template of Prime Ministers confirms this. Here is what appears under the caption of *Legacy* for Prime Minister Patterson (the highlight is mine):

> *Jamaica's most successful politician at national level, breaking the 'third-term' barrier.* His style of leadership is not to rely on fiery rhetoric, but on fundamental principles of procedure. He has done more than any other political leader to date, to empower his associates and to structure a party committed [to] negotiate peace and settle differences through a reconciling process rather than confrontation. His wide experience at national, regional and international level, as a negotiator, has served him well in office as Prime Minister.

Taking the duration of service as Prime Minister as a hallmark of performance is a most deficient measure of the effectiveness of any national leader. Yet, the sad truth is that this is among the most prevalent of measures of political success in nearly all Third World countries, from Angola (Eduardo dos Santos) to Zimbabwe (Robert Mugabe). To be fair, the attributed legacy of Prime Minister Seaga is only marginally more flattering (again the highlight is mine):

> Local constituency organization and national cultural development are two areas of particular achievement for Edward Seaga. **For forty years was successful in a constituency that no other politician was able to hold for more than five years.** His transformation of depressed inner-city areas within his West Kingston constituency, into vibrant communities, made him the unrivalled king of constituency transformation in Jamaica. Culturally, he was the nation's leading pioneer of ideas and institutions to promote culture, nationally and internationally.

It would not be surprising if it were discovered that both these Prime Ministers took umbrage at their ascribed legacies, especially taking into account the source of the accreditation – the information arm of the government of Jamaica. This would be clearly understandable, naturally. After all, even they themselves must see this summary of their contributions as wanting. Any disagreement on the soundness or fairness of the summary of their legacies may not be entirely uncalled-for. However, there is no escaping the reality that a credible source of commentary on matters such as this, recognizes the attributes ascribed to be the most extraordinary elements of a summary of their professional careers. It is a very telling revelation that appears to validate the contention that the more things change the more they remain the same. I would hazard a guess that neither Prime Minister will ever attain a status that could warrant him being considered for elevation to the level of national hero.

During the period from 1983 to 2006 I returned to Jamaica at least once each year. I was always struck by a number of relatively simple things that seemed disproportionately symptomatic of Jamaica's plight. Among the most memorable of these were school age children scurrying about near nightfall in places like Cross Roads and Halfway Tree trying to find transportation home after school; the alarming number of idle post-secondary school age young people who just sat around in many urban areas seemingly bereft of occupation, hope or purpose; the indescribable, nearly all-day traffic jams everywhere in the corporate area of Kingston and lower St. Andrew; the clear indication that an unusually large and growing number of people had decided that to become *informal traders* (a clever euphemism for the commonly used but pejorative term, *higgler)* was not simply the best way in which to earn a living, given their circumstances, but the only way. In fact, the informal trading sector now accounts for about 40% of Jamaica's GDP. I confided to a number of friends on each of my visits how alarming these symptoms were. I indicated that in very many respects they were identical to the symptoms of endless decline that I witnessed in many cities and towns in Africa. Indeed, they raised identical concerns and fears in my mind because of what they portend, given the outcomes visible all over the African continent.

Most troubling of all on my visits, however, was the disengagement of Prime Minister Patterson. His presence was never seen or felt in either a purely political sense or in a manner indicative of his being in charge of, or even simply overseeing, the major aspects of the nation's business. Even supporters of his in the Private Sector Organization of Jamaica (PSOJ) expressed concern at his obvious detachment. Over time the Prime Minister's behavior seemed to graduate from mere detachment to virtual absence from the national scene. In fact, I often joked with friends who were known supporters of his that were I simply a foreign visitor to Jamaica I would not have been able to tell who was the country's leader since he was both silent and invisible.

My own summary of the period is that it was a period of the purest exercise of *laissez faire* excess ever witnessed in the entire Caribbean. A number of businessmen of my acquaintance agreed with this assessment. While appreciative of the unusual degree of non-intervention of the government in their business affairs, they were deeply concerned at the potential for increasingly abusive behavior on the part of the business elite that saw only opportunity but no obligation regarding the welfare of the working class or the nation at large. The performance of the local economy during the period as reflected in Douglas Orane's earlier commentary is further confirmed in the table below. This is based on details from the **World Bank Report** *(pp.44 – 45)*.

How Jamaica Compares Internationally on Average Real GDP Growth

Years	1960-69	1970-79	1980-89	1990-99	2000-2008
Jamaica	4.4	1.2	1.7	2.3	1.3
Ranking *	72/118	128/132	129/170	119/193	180/196
Ranking **	18/27	29/31	20/33	26/34	29/34

*Global (ranking/number of countries)

**Regional: Latin America and the Caribbean (ranking/number of countries)

Jamaica was one of the world's slowest growing economies in the past four decades. Jamaica also fell behind most of its per capita income peers. Comparing Jamaica with its closest 19 peers in per capita GDP shows that the country lost ground. Between1970 and 2008, Jamaica's real per capita GDP growth was 13% and its rank within this group of 20 countries fell from 7th to 18th. This growth rate is the lowest in the entire group.

During the period both governments and Prime Ministers changed but with no net positive outcomes for the national economy nor verifiable improvement in the quality of life for the vast majority of citizens. Unfortunately, this will continue to be the case until and unless there are changes in how we view and approach our problems and indeed our vision as a people and nation. If we do not awaken to this reality we should be prepared to endure increasingly difficult times. But we do have choices on some of the most critical issues affecting our personal and national welfare: our government, our leaders and our own personal vision of how we picture ourselves and our country in the future. It is said that there is no greater motivation than our vision of ourselves in the future. It is also said that without vision the people perish.

g. The Trifecta: Choice, Consequence & Responsibility

Both consequence and responsibility arise inevitably from the choices we make either as individuals or as a nation. While we are aware of the link and understand the relationships instinctively, we tend not to remain engaged constantly with these relationships. Perhaps this accounts, in large measure, for our inability, unwillingness or reluctance to assign blame or to hold political parties or leaders accountable. Regardless, the durable truth is that consequence remains indifferent to our recognition or admission of its cause. In the same vein, we all suffer the pain of its impact. Neither indifference nor denial can save us. So the question becomes: how do we change our behavior and so empower ourselves to respond to our circumstances in a manner that confidently confronts the *status quo*, clearly improves the chances of meeting national objectives and visibly expands opportunity for the majority of our citizens?

The vast majority of us may already know the answer to the question since the answer is clearly self-evident: we must acknowledge that we are active agents of choice and therefore responsible for the choices we make. If this is the case we cannot deny that we are also active agents of change and likewise unavoidably responsible for the outcomes realized; those that place us on the escalator and uplift as well as those that force us into the crevice and distress. One is left to wonder why it is that we sit like frogs in a large beaker of hot water on a Bunsen burner blithely adjusting to the progressively increasing temperature even unto the point of near death. The available evidence seems to indicate that we have been making adjustments in one direction only – the direction of accommodation. Instead, we need to move decisively in the direction of confrontation and rejection. Surely, at this point in our history we should have come to understand that continuous accommodation of the *status quo* will not ever bring about the future we claim to seek: *"Jamaica, the place of choice to live, work, raise families and do business"* **(The Vision Statement in the National Development Plan for Jamaica,** now commonly known as **Vision 2030 Jamaica** or simply, **Vision 2030).**

It is worthwhile to validate the extent of the impact of the trifecta of choice, consequence and responsibility. In my lifetime I am able to recall only a single clear, positive demonstration of this relationship on a matter of national significance:

the entry by Jamaica into the ill-fated West Indies Federation in 1958, the subsequent Referendum that resulted in Jamaica exiting the union in 1961 and the most extraordinary, honorable, unequivocal acceptance of responsibility for this outcome by the then Premier, Norman Washington Manley. At the time Manley believed with all his heart that the Federation was the very best political arrangement for Jamaica and the other nine Anglophone territories that supported this view. In this belief Manley actively chose to take Jamaica into the Federation. He campaigned relentlessly for national acceptance of his position after disagreements arose among the major partners in the venture and after his rival and cousin, Alexander Bustamante, launched a blistering campaign against Jamaica remaining in the Federation.

In her award winning biography, **Drumblair,** *Memories Of A Jamaican Childhood,* Rachel Manley, Norman Manley's granddaughter, relates in great detail how torn her grandfather was between his profound desire for Independence and his determination that Federation was a necessity. Yet, when the very foundation of the Federation came into question he voluntarily and immediately put the question of whether or not to remain in the union to the people. The very instructive fact is that having just won the preceding general elections he could have postponed the exercise for an entire election cycle or perhaps longer. Once again, Manley actively chose to act in keeping with his conviction of what was the right thing to do. Interestingly, his son Michael, Rachel's father, took a somewhat Machiavellian approach in opposition to his father's decision. Rachel quotes her father as saying (p. 239), *"I'm not sure I agree with you. I mean, you just won the most spectacular landslide. You don't have to stretch democracy that far! All you have to do is use their* [the electorate's] *goodwill and keep selling them the new deal. Busta* [Alexander Bustamante] *can't do anything till the next election, and that buys you enough time."*

The elder Manley, as we know, held the referendum and lost. The major personal and national consequence of this outcome was an early general election since such a significant loss at the polls made it just about mandatory to seek a vote of confidence from the electorate. Manley lost this vote of confidence election as well. He never once equivocated about either his rationale for his actions or for the defeats he suffered. Instead, he readily acknowledged both losses and accepted full personal responsibility for all related outcomes. I am unable to recall any similar demonstration of integrity in our political history that even comes close to that displayed here. Consider as well the fact that Norman Manley refused to accept the traditional knighthood on account of what appears to be an understandable conflict in his own mind between being one's own man and being a permanent, walking representative or agent of a monarchy about which he must have had fundamental misgivings in principle. Alexander Bustamante had no qualm accepting knighthood. If one can be truly politically selfless, Norman Manley's response to the personal and national circumstances he faced exemplifies a level of integrity that is seldom witnessed among politicians anywhere. Unfortunately, in the context of today's politics his response would doubtlessly be considered political suicide. For this reason such a response would never be considered.

For comparison, let us look at the alarming choices and unfavorable consequences attached to the involvement of former Prime Minister Bruce Golding in the Christopher Coke affair. At the time, and certainly in retrospect, Golding was faced with the most significant tipping point of his political life. The political landscape of Jamaica was also ready for courageous re-ordering. The subsequent sequence of events will validate the inescapability of the choice, consequence, and responsibility trifecta.

Golding chose to accept the Tivoli Gardens constituency as the seat that would most easily ensure his achieving the position of Prime Minister. Surely, there were less problematic alternatives although none as certain of success. For example, he could have declined the constituency by switching with a sitting member of parliament in a secure JLP seat. Even were we to assume that Golding did not have a relationship with Coke prior to his accepting the constituency, there can be no doubt that once he accepted the constituency a working relationship with Coke was inevitable. Knowing the implications of this inevitability it is not unreasonable to think that a sensitive and wise Prime Minister-in-waiting would consider alternative options, especially given the very high expectations he had led so many to believe he could and would meet. He vocalized the major concerns and fears of a significant majority of the middle class in the areas of crime and corruption and inveighed against these maladies incessantly with righteous vigor and conviction. He should have seen the pitfalls awaiting him in Tivoli. He exercised the easiest but poorest of judgments by his choice. The consequences would eventually lead to the premature ending of his political career and further advance the widespread belief that the Tivoli garrison, as well as all other garrisons for that matter, was impregnable and sacrosanct.

Golding enjoyed the support and intense goodwill of Jamaicans at home and abroad at a time when Jamaicans yearned for a potential savior that would lead the country out of the wasteland of crime, corruption and declining productivity. His political pedigree, intellect, experience and campaigning certainly engendered such faith and hope. No other politician on the scene at the time even came close to matching the promising package that Golding seemed to embody. In combination with the obvious opportunities this presented, there was no doubt that the time was ripe for taking Jamaica on a new course; one that offered the promise of dramatic reduction in crime and corruption and a return to steady, even if slow, growth in productivity. Indeed, the forces were aligned to create a critical opportunity not just for the Prime Minister himself but for the nation as a whole.

Up to this point there had never been as favorable a prospect for bold action to address the single, most malicious scourge facing Jamaica – crime and its known association with politics. More than any of his predecessors Golding was presented with an enormous opportunity with extraordinary potential to make an historic difference. He was fresh to the position, he was highly regarded, and he had no significant political baggage that would hinder his being audacious. There was no visible reason why he should not succeed.

As Prime Minister, Golding appeared ready to do what everyone hoped and expected that he would. He appeared to be willing to reverse the trend of the increasing ascendancy of criminal elements in the conduct of political affairs in the country. It was therefore very heartening to the majority of Jamaicans when the security forces were given permission to enter Tivoli Gardens, Jamaica's quintessential garrison and

Golding's own constituency. In order to understand and appreciate the monumental significance of this step we must consider the following excerpt from a Mark Wignall article in the **Jamaica Observer of May 30, 2010**:

> *To the typical policeman and soldier, in times of conflict, Tivoli Gardens is a community to be feared.*
>
> *In most of the previous confrontations there has been an almost tacit understanding that the security forces remain outside the perimeter of the community, surrounding it on all sides, on the east, north and south on Darling Street, full south on Marcus Garvey Drive, west on Industrial Terrace and from the north, the main operations are usually centred at Denham Town Police Station.*
>
> *But the understanding seems to be accepted by the Tivoli gunmen too, who remain in the inner periphery of Tivoli Gardens. So while the madness takes place, the security forces pelt Tivoli Gardens with gunfire while the gunmen in Tivoli hit back with assistance from their compatriots in Denham Town. After a few days and a few more dead bodies, both sides pack it up and this crazy country returns to 'normality'.*
>
> *Easily the most heavily armed and well-organised garrison community, Tivoli was always an area difficult to breach and it is nigh on impossible to carry out 'search and destroy' missions for gunmen because gunfire may come from a window while inside that particular room behind the window may be old men, women and children.*
>
> *It is my belief that Tivoli Gardens never expected that the army would have entered with such force.*

Wignall's reporting is corroborated by what is perhaps the most extensive exposé of the Tivoli Gardens incident, **A Massacre in Jamaica,** by Mattathias

Schwartz. The story appeared in **The New Yorker, December 12, 2011**. Schwartz reveals the momentous nature of what was being attempted by Golding. The excerpt below is instructive:

> *After the United States demanded the extradition of a drug lord, a blood-letting ensued.*
>
> *The trouble that led to the Tivoli Gardens deaths began in August, 2009, when the United States government requested the extradition of Christopher (Dudus) Coke. In the U.S., Coke stood charged in federal court of trafficking in narcotics and firearms; in Jamaica, he was known as the country's most powerful "don," a community leader who also runs a criminal enterprise. He lived in Tivoli, where everyone called him "president," and, since 2001, Jamaican police had not been able to enter the neighborhood without his permission. Coke was so powerful that Prime Minister Bruce Golding spent months resisting the extradition order. But in early May, 2010, under heavy international political pressure, Golding authorized Coke's arrest. In response, Coke converted Tivoli and nearby Denham Town into a personal fortress. Barricades of rubble and barbed wire sprang up across major intersections. Armed sentries took up posts around Tivoli's perimeter. It looked as though Coke were preparing for war with the Jamaican state.*

It is now very easy to see why the Prime Minister's actions stimulated the hope that finally one of the root causes of rampant crime and community disloca-tion in Jamaica was about to be dealt a terminal blow. It stands to reason that if Golding could approve such an assault on his own constituency no other garrison community was immune from a similar fate. In fact, it is rumored that a number of dons from other garrison communities voluntarily surrendered to the police during the period of the invasion of Tivoli, mainly out of fear for their own lives. It appears that none was detained. The death toll from the Tivoli engagement is officially documented as seventy four of which one casualty is a soldier. Not surprisingly, there is widespread belief that the total number of casualties is grossly understated.

Following the national realization of the human cost of the Tivoli Gardens foray and the questionable professionalism of the security forces, Golding himself faltered and became progressively a casualty of events that both his actions and the response of others to these actions unleashed. Many were also astounded at his hesitancy or unwillingness to expand the assault to all the other garrison communities. One major consequential event was the call for his resignation by the architect of Tivoli Gardens himself, Edward Seaga, the former Prime Minister and erstwhile leader of the JLP.

The Wignall article comments on this insertion of Seaga into the developing controversy:

> Now that Seaga has spoken and has said that Golding should resign, the popular sentiment will gain traction, not because Seaga is popular, but because Golding is so disliked at this time.

> One woman wrote, "I still cannot recover from the disappointment in Mr. Golding. I maintain that he should resign. I notice that he is being hit from left, right and center. In the short run, he will not be able to stand the heat and will resign. In fairness to him, though, he did not create Tivoli, he inherited it. In all of this bangarang, you journalists have allowed Eddie Seaga, the architect of this fiefdom, to escape free. Tivoli community is the creation of Edward Seaga and he is to take most if not all of the blame for the bangarang."

In the end, Coke was apprehended and ultimately extradited, tried and sentenced to 23 years in jail in America; the Public Defender was tasked to investigate and report on all the circumstances surrounding the invasion of Tivoli Gardens. (It is now more than two years since the invasion of Tivoli Gardens and the Public Defender's report is yet to be presented.) The Prime Minister resigned, thus accepting responsibility for the

Tivoli Gardens tragedy. The unavoidable question is why did Golding's judgment fail so dreadfully at the moment of greatest opportunity to change the trajectory of Jamaica's politics dramatically? It is a question that only he may be able to answer conclusively. I doubt that the question has ever been asked of him directly. In the meantime, it surely is a question that we must attempt to answer ourselves with or without his contribution.

Both the powerful and those who aspire to power appear committed to varying degrees of flexibility in regard to truth and honor. Most often their rule of truth and honor is guided by the maxim that the end justifies the means. Accordingly, the extent to which truth and honor are sacrificed depends on the assessed value of the end being sought. In the case of the Prime Minister he seems to have placed such exceptional value in preserving the affection of his constituents, especially that of the community bene-factor Christopher Coke, that he decided to sacrifice the truth and his honor so dispro-portionately that his popularity and goodwill were also sacrificed. At this stage nothing could save him from the contempt of those he took an oath to serve. In the world of politics there can be no greater fall from grace. In fact, the Prime Minister's stature had so diminished that during the Manatt-Dudus hearing on the Christopher Coke extradi-tion matter he was treated with scant respect by the cross examining attorney, Queen's Counsel K. D. Knight, who accused the Prime Minister of being *pathologically menda-cious*. In a manner of speaking, if the emperor had been fully clothed before the hearing he was stark naked by its end. There is a life lesson to be learnt from all of this: personal integrity is most severely tested at the intersection of opportunity and judgment. In political affairs this intersection is consistently the site of the most tragic of disasters.

The efficacy of the trifecta has been demonstrated in both favorable and unfa-vorable personal and national circumstances. It clearly shows that when judgment is impaired, especially on account of predominantly personal, partisan consider-ations, both truth and honor are at great risk and leadership is at best tentative and at worst absent completely. It appears to me that this failure in judgment and lead-ership may actually have increased the degree of difficulty in effectively addressing the matter of garrisons in Jamaica in the future.

3

INDEPENDENCE AFTERGLOW

a. The Irony of Legacy

It is incontestable that 1962, the year of Independence, marks a watershed in the history of Jamaica. Similarly, there is no doubt that there is much irony in the reality that the newly independent nation embraced wholeheartedly the very two-party-system-democracy that was the instrument of our subjugation for more than 300 years. Remarkably, it did so purposely without coercion, question, or controversy.

In retrospect one finds it difficult not to wonder why a political system that justified slavery, relegated an entire population to the status of lesser beings, shamelessly compensated former slave owners to the tune of nearly US$20 billion (current value) for their *loss of property* with nary a consideration of compensating the nearly 700,000 former slaves for their forced servitude, could or should ever be worthy of adulation and emulation by those it exploited mercilessly and, in some cases up to this day, without remorse. This quiet surrender of an entire people has to be seen as one of the most glaring examples of the ever controversial Stockholm Syndrome that afflicts those who embrace their captors and abusers as honorable and support the very philosophy used by these oppressors to justify the general elimination of their freedom. Even at this distance from ground zero the humiliation of the subterfuge continues to have palpable effect on how we see ourselves as well as in our behavior to one another. Of equal concern, of course, is the fact that the system continues to be revered by many as the very best form of government possible. To understand the hubris of those who support the system unquestionably we simply need to consider Winston Churchill's contention that *"Democracy is the worst form of Government except all those other forms that have been tried from time to time."*

It is not without significance that highly reputable figures in Caribbean society are currently and justifiably raising the matter of reparations for slavery and giving the lie to the vaunted claims of the unique virtues of Democracy. For example, Caribbean economic historian, Sir Hilary Beckles' new book, **Britain's Black Debt: Reparations for Caribbean Slavery and Native Genocide,** addresses the issue extensively. A directly relevant excerpt from the April 12, 2013 issue of the online news service, **Caribbean 360,** is worth repeating here:

> *Except for the blindest and unrelenting apologists for the acts of genocide and enslavement, it is impossible to discard Beckles' assertion that these were "crimes against humanity". As he says: "The wealth of the (British) Empire required the abandonment of all known laws, conventions, moral parameters, political practices and legal frameworks and the creation of a new and unprecedented labour system".*

The distressing certainty of the claims concerning the virtues of Democracy forces us to return to the earlier point of the possible irretrievability of the opportunity that faced both Norman Manley and Alexander Bustamante at the very outset of the formation of the respective Jamaican political parties: the possible creation of a government of unity and not a government of definitively competitive or permanently adversarial forces. After all, Bustamante was initially a member of the PNP. This past opportunity may be past but not necessarily irretrievable. We will explore this possibility at length later in our journey toward contemplating a more reliably effective way in which to address our problems.

It is not without pertinence and significance, and perhaps prescient, that on February 26, 2013 the island of Grenada has in effect become for a second time the only single-party democracy in the Caribbean after freely electing representatives of the New National Party (NNP) to all 15 available seats in the government. The people purposely and, it should be noted, democratically, eliminated the so-called loyal opposition.

In spite of the automatic credit given to two-party-system-democracy, the evidence of Jamaica's lack of positive progress under this regime since Independence should make us question its status as a uniquely progressive political system that deserves automatic acceptance as the most likely to effectively facilitate individual and national advancement.

We may refer once again to the Orane address to the CIN and the **World Bank Report,** to at least question this assertion or perhaps to openly conclude otherwise. In one of the most scholarly and compelling books related to politics, the changing patterns and distribution of power and scarce resources in Jamaica, **Demeaned but Empowered**: *The Social Power of the Urban Poor in Jamaica*, Obika Gray aptly designates the two-party-system-democracy a *political cartel*. This designation appears to imply either profound disenchantment with the system or an acknowledgement that the system has been co-opted for the purpose of self-aggrandizement by tacit agreement between the two political parties. In either case this supports the contention that the system is seriously flawed and is unlikely to live up to its promise or the expectations of those it claims to serve.

Even in the United States of America democracy is under assault from political forces at both ends of the political spectrum – the so-called Far Right and Far Left. The one is bent on transforming traditional democracy into rule by supporters of the irascible, strict constitutional constructionists; the other places very great weight on an egalitarian morality that sees elitism, gross class differentiation and severe income inequality as direct consequences of the behavior of the Far Right and as instruments of not so subtle discrimination and oppression. It is fair to say, especially after the most recent presidential elections, that the majority of Americans sees the most acceptable path to progress somewhere in between these extremes. This explains why membership in both the Democratic and Republican parties continues to decline and the number of those that identify as Independents continues to increase. In fact, the latter group now polls at above 40% of the voting population.

It should be plain to all that just as our lives are works in progress, it is a necessity that the instruments by which we manage and direct our lives reflect this reality. Those irrationally committed to the *status quo* attempt to insulate themselves from the discomfort occasioned by the relentless nature of change by demanding that things remain the same. In America, these citizens tend to adhere to the very strictest and most simplistic, self-serving interpretations of both the Constitution and the Christian Bible in order to make their point. This, without doubt, is the faultiest of thinking since both the Constitution and the Bible have been subjected to changes in interpretation, subsequent amendment and revision. More directly to the point, there can be no doubt whatsoever that the Amendments to the United States Constitution, for example, represent the most admirable attempts to make America a *more perfect union*. This is usually the intent of sensible, meaningful, humanistic political philosophy.

In the meantime it may be of value to look at a country that gained its independence from our common British colonial masters in 1959, three years earlier than Jamaica. While there is certainly a number of cultural distinctions that make Singapore singular in nature in comparison to Jamaica, notably the greater homogeneity of its people, both colonies were subjected to almost identical subjugation but for the element of slavery. Singapore even entered the federal system of the Federation of Malaysia but was expelled by the Federation for mainly cultural and economic reasons after just two years. Singapore subsequently became a parliamentary republic in 1965. The country eventually devised a path that was somewhere between a democracy and a dictatorship under the extraordinary leadership of Lee Kuan Yew. Kuan Yew was no less disappointed by the failure of his attempt at federation than was our own Norman Manley at Jamaica's own failed attempt. However, Kuan Yew found a path that was identical in intent but markedly different in practice. He expressed his anguish and intentions in a single statement (the bold print is mine):

> *"For me, it is a moment of anguish. All my life ... I believed in Malaysian merger and unity of the two territories. You know that we, as a people, are connected by geography, economics, by ties of kinship ... It literally broke everything that we stood for ... now* **Singapore shall be forever a sovereign democratic and independent nation, founded upon the principles of liberty and justice and ever seeking the welfare and happiness of the people in a most and just equal society."**

The outcomes from Kuan Yew's efforts at developing his country are exemplary. Singapore is greatly admired by the vast majority of observers in spite of the fact that Kuan Yew very cleverly abandoned the traditional concept of democracy to which he appeared deeply committed initially. The chosen course has nevertheless yielded all if not more than the hoped for benefits of standard capitalistic democracy. Of course, the Singapore model has its critics and detractors. This is due primarily to its impure democratic practices. Still, these critics and detractors face a massive conundrum on a couple of incontestable grounds: in the first case the citizens of Singapore themselves freely admit to loving their system of government; in the second, the country's successes on both the economic and social fronts are acknowledged as phenomenal by the experts that monitor such things.

In order to better appreciate both the conundrum and Singapore's undeniably remarkable progress we may observe excerpts from two reports: the **December 2012 Democracy Audit World Report** and the **2013 Index of Economic Freedom from The Heritage Foundation in Partnership with Wall Street Journal.** In the first case a smaller number is the preferred score. One cannot help but focus on the Corruption Index in the table, especially as it is the only item in the entire table that provides Singapore with an advantage over Jamaica. This index indicates that Jamaica is thirteen times more corrupt than Singapore. We need to keep this in mind as we proceed.

DEMOCRACY AUDIT		JAMAICA	SINGAPORE
Topics	Range	Ranking	Ranking
World Democracy Audit overall ranking	1-150	40	71
Political Rights	1-7	2	4
Civil Liberties	1-7	3	4
Press Freedom	0-150	12	110
Corruption	0-149	65	5

The Heritage Foundation commentary confirms the preeminence of Singapore as an overall success story and ranks the country second only to Hong Kong in its overall rankings. Commentary on Jamaica is also provided for comparison. I have emphasized what I consider quite interesting and critical aspects of the commentary.

On Singapore:

*Singapore is a **nominally democratic state** that has been ruled by the People's Action Party (PAP) since independence in 1965. The PAP won the May 2010 elections with the lowest percentage of the popular vote in its history. Six opposition members also won seats. Certain civil liberties, such as freedom of assembly and freedom of speech, remain restricted, but the PAP has embraced economic liberalization and international trade. **Singapore is one of the world's most prosperous nations. Its economy is dominated by services, but the country is also a major manufacturer of electronics and chemicals***

On Jamaica:

Prime Minister Portia Simpson Miller's People's National Party took office in January 2012 with a large parliamentary majority and is expected to maintain market-friendly policies. **High interest rates and excessive government debt burden the economy.** *A USD$1.27 billion Standby Agreement with the International Monetary Fund for balance of payment support, signed in 2010, required major fiscal reforms that have been slow to materialize. Services account for more than 60 percent of GDP. Most foreign exchange comes from remittances, tourism, and bauxite, all of which declined sharply in the 2009 recession. Tourism receipts have recovered slightly. Unemployment and underemployment in the formal sector are high.* **Violent crime, fueled by the drug trade, is a serious problem.**

There can be no doubt that there are alternative paths to national viability that do not require excessively mindless commitment to traditional two-party-system-democracy. The inescapable question is the extent to which we value the process of governing via this system versus alternative systems that are more likely to provide the outcomes upon which traditional two-party-system-democracy is predicated but which it seldom, if ever, delivers. After all, the Singapore model clearly delivers outcomes that contribute reliably to the well-being of the citizenry and the nation as an enduring enterprise. This is a concern that must be given much greater thought, examination and analysis by Jamaica and its citizens with much more than academic curiosity or fleeting popular interest. This concern also enhances the legitimacy of the questioning of the automatic, unquestionable acceptance of two-party-system-democracy by our leaders and the vast majority of our people. Note how in the above comment on Jamaica the expectation that the government will maintain *market-friendly policies* obviously takes precedence over the government's responsibility to assure the personal security of the population in the face of acknowledged criminality. We will reflect on this troubling but seemingly natural failing of two-party-system-democracy separately.

To be fair, Michael Manley is perhaps singular in his attempt to make adjustments to this template but was extremely challenged managerially and went too far out of balance to win the long-term tolerance if not the support of a large number of Jamaicans as well as First World power brokers. This attempted departure from the *status quo* remains a matter of much discourse these many years after the fact and is mentioned in a financial commentary by Wilberne Persaud in his column in the **Daily Gleaner** of January 8, 2010. Persaud observes:

> *Manley's humanity and vision, struggle for equity and justice are all indisputable. Mechanisms of attainment, however, obviously failed; so have successors of both parties. Our current situation seems no better. There appears to be blurred vision, an absence of thoughtful and structured communication.*

> *2010 requires we seek that cohesion among diverse and often contradictory elements of our society whose objectives, once coordinated, might achieve harmony alongside democracy.*

Of all our post-Independence political leaders, Michael Manley was by far the most effectively disruptive of *the status quo*. Regrettably, he was positively successful, in terms of outcomes, almost solely in the area of what may be described as social engineering. The following excerpt from an earlier work, **Jamaican by Birth American by Choice**, explains:

> *His most transformative legacy is in the social and legislative reforms he implemented in Jamaica. These include a National Minimum Wage, Maternity Leave with Pay, ….. a National Literacy Program and the Status of Children Act which ended discrimination against children born out of wedlock. (p. 52)*

> *The social reforms which Manley implemented were a watershed in the area of social mobility in Jamaica. ….. no observant commentator can*

deny that Manley awakened in the average Jamaican an unshakable and profound belief that his time had come and that he had every right to expect equal opportunity at upward mobility in Jamaican society. (p. 54)

Unfortunately, Manley was unfavorably disruptive in the area of national economics. His introduction of a Bauxite Levy along with his attempt to create an international bauxite cartel incurred the punitive wrath of the United States. Generally, his insensitivity, and perhaps indifference, to the concerns of the United States and the local business community triggered the most harmful exodus of the professional and entrepreneurial classes in the history of modern Jamaica. In a number of respects, the effects of this exodus are still evident today. Notwithstanding all this, Manley is considered a visionary and is without doubt one of the most remarkable figures in the post-colonial period of Jamaica and the entire English speaking Caribbean.

In one of his last interviews Manley expressed regret that he was not more sensitive to the financial costs of the social programs he implemented as these affected the overall national budget. This confirms the fact that addressing the *status quo* is not without cost and requires the recognition that there are always competing demands against a very limited national budget. Also evident and equally vital on this account is the clear need for effective leadership.

The Persaud article referenced earlier also comments on Kuan Yew and some of Kuan Yew's observations about Jamaica after Kuan Yew's visit in 1975:

Lee Kuan Yew's opponents in Singapore claimed he operated with an iron fist, generally with no velvet glove.

Undoubtedly, Jamaicans would not warm to such an approach.

Nevertheless class, race, colour and other divisions must be understood and 'managed' if not overcome, for sustainable development. Jamaica's developmental problem cannot be simplistically subsumed under categories like interest and exchange rates or, in general, the economy.

*The form Jamaican capitalism takes must be capable of overcoming poten-
tially destructive conflict embedded in our specific 'history and necessities'.*

*Educated Caribbean youth understand Lee Kuan Yew telling his successor
generation that public order, personal security, social progress and prosperity are not the natural order of things.*

*They know honest and effective government can deliver, but despair. They
feel powerless and dejected.*

*Honesty and effectiveness of government and private sector supporters are
absent among the cadre of modern successors to anti-colonial national-
ists who struggled for independence. This is a core opinion discernible
throughout the region.*

The most insightful observation in the statement above may easily be overlooked
but should not be: *The form Jamaican capitalism takes must be capable of overcoming potentially destructive conflict embedded in our specific 'history and necessities'.* This must be
top of mind when we come to question more directly our wholehearted acceptance
of our inherited two-party-system-democracy. It is all but impossible not to focus
on the first two sentences in the quote as well: *Lee Kuan Yew's opponents in Singapore
claimed he operated with an iron fist, generally with no velvet glove. Undoubtedly, Jamaicans
would not warm to such an approach.* As much as anything else, this is demonstrative of Jamaica's dilemma. The supporters of traditional Democracy abhor the *iron
fist* approach except, perhaps, when practiced by an accepted oppressor, but this
approach, or something close to this approach, is perhaps what is needed at this
juncture in Jamaica's history as long as the dysfunctional political parties remain
unwilling to see that commitment to *country first* is by far a more promising obligation than commitment to *party and politician* above all else.

There is an elaborately constructed piece of humor about Jamaicans in circula-
tion on the Internet. Like native music and art, such pieces of humor go directly to

the generally perceived character of Jamaicans. This piece of humor is worthy of reproduction here because it so powerfully exemplifies the monumental indifference of far too many Jamaicans to the matter of indiscipline and unwillingness to conform or to accommodate change beyond that which is immediately self-serving. The origin of the piece is unknown:

> *St. Peter came to the Lord and said, "Lord, I have to talk to you. I have a problem. I know we didn't have many Jamaicans in heaven so you instituted an affirmative action plan and we are supposed to have 10,000 Jamaicans in heaven. But they are causing so many problems! They have torn down the Pearly Gates by swinging on them. They have let in another 10,000 of their bredrin through the fence. They are constantly standing by the gate disturbing Angel Gabriel, begging for a 'bly' for their baby modder, cousin, sistren, neighbour, granny, auntie....*

> *Whenever it is their turn to watch the gates they keep letting in good looking women and fat women. They have stolen my harp. They have gotten jerk sauce all over their white robes. Drum pan chicken is being sold all over the Streets of Gold. Some are walking around with only one wing because they are 'styling'. Angels must have two wings to fly! Some of them have put on chrome wings that dazzle the other angels when they are flying. The white robes are eternal and must be washed five times a day. Some haven't washed their robes since they arrived because they didn't come to heaven to do 'day's work'. Some have refused to take their turn in helping keep the Stairway to Heaven clean because 'dem ah nuh nobody helper'. Many who came here because they used salt are still using it because they don't like 'ital' food. Some refuse to wear their halos because they don't fit right over their hairstyles. Others are wearing their halos as necklaces. Others are wearing their halos with the tags still attached to them for 'stylie'. Others have discarded the white halos and are wearing gold ones instead. They claim these are 'bashy'.*

Most of the women have discarded their white robes and are wearing white shorts and 'batty riders' claiming that they have pretty skin and want to show off their 'bandy legs'. Reggae music is blasted at all hours of night at their 'bashments', disturbing all the other residents. Their cellular phones are worn on their robes and keep ringing during prayers. Recently there was an altercation between Adam and one Jamaican who claims he was only 'checking out' Eve. They have planted marijuana in the Garden of Eden since the soil is so fertile, claiming 'man and man haffi hustle'. What should I do?"

The Lord said, "It wouldn't be fair to not let Jamaicans in heaven. They have just as much right to be here as other nationalities. Maybe we just don't know how to deal with them; maybe we are using the wrong approach. We need to check with someone who has more experience dealing with them. Let's call the Devil."

The Devil answered the phone and said, "Hello, Lord. What can I do for you?" The Lord said, "We have a problem up here, and we'd like to talk to you about it." The Devil said, "Just a minute, I've got to put you on hold." The Devil was gone five minutes. He came back to the phone and said, "OK Lord, I'm back. What's up?" The Lord said, "Well, I would like to talk to you about a problem up here." Once again the Devil excused himself and put the Lord on hold. This time he was gone for fifteen minutes. Finally, the Devil came back to the phone and said, "Lord, I am really sorry, but I can't talk to you right now. I have to go. These damn Jamaicans down here..... Yesterday they had air conditioning installed. Now they have just extinguished Hell's Fire, saying 'man come to Hell fe chill'."

As is often the case, many a truth is said in jest.

b. Deficits in Leadership

We have dramatically devalued some useful aspects of the currency of our fateful inheritance. The excerpt, **My Country 'Tis for Thee,** from the earlier mentioned work, **Brackets**, laments the fact.

> *Could it be we are out of time?*
> *Is triage permanent territory*
> *Hostile to rhythm and rhyme?*
> *Promise and hope now paltry*
> *Fail to stem patricidal crime.*
> *Sadness yields to the mourning*
> *Insistent reality demands.*
> *There is no trace of morning*
> *As resolute, lonely evening stands*
> *In the shambles of our declining.*
>
> *'Born fi dead' not just sons and daughters*
> *But the very soul of nineteen sixty two.*
> *Lament the tale but confront our fathers.*
> *Not so many but yet a remarkable few,*
> *Complicit in the crafting of disasters.*
> *It used to be the abyss loomed*
> *Only now and maybe with regret*
> *There is no abyss just the doomed.*
> *Impostors, leaders made erect*
> *Disheveled intentions never groomed.*

Despite the misgivings expressed about the inherited two-party-system-democracy, we did inherit some very useful administrative tools and systems from the British. Among the most noteworthy are the technocracy or, as we know it generally, the Civil Service, and the structure and practice of an effective system of education. Taken together these are undoubtedly formidable legacies that would allow a fledgling nation not to flounder either internally or in its dealings with others. This certainly was the case for at least the first decade of Independence. In retrospect, we realize that this period was merely a memorable, intoxicating honeymoon. The hangover would follow. Regrettably, it is a hangover from which we are yet to recover.

Economic growth of about 6% per annum marked the first ten years of independence under a JLP government led successively by Prime Ministers Alexander Bustamante, Donald Sangster and Hugh Shearer. This group presided over the most tranquil days of the post-Independence period. Perhaps this tranquility was less their own doing than the good fortune of being honeymooners. The growth was fuelled by strong investments in bauxite/alumina, tourism, the manufacturing industry and, to a lesser extent, the agricultural sector.

In his presentation, **Management, Economic Development And Caribbean Corporate Leadership,** to the Caribbean Corporate Leadership Conference in Barbados in 2007, Sir Courtney Blackman, Former Barbados Ambassador to the USA and the OAS, introduced his address with a most telling observation:

> *"This Paper takes off from the late Peter Drucker's penetrating insight that* **'economic and social development, above all, means management,'** *and its corollary that* **'there are no underdeveloped countries, only under-managed ones.'** *It is a sobering thought that in the early 1960s the economic prospects of the British West Indies appeared far rosier than those countries which we call the Asian tigers — Hong Kong, Singapore, South Korea and Taiwan. But whereas the Tigers have recorded annual growth rates of six to ten per cent over the last three decades, most Caribbean states have experienced only modest economic growth rates while some of them, notably Guyana and Jamaica, have actually regressed."*

In a single paragraph Sir Courtney manages to reflect the nature of the basic failure of post-Independence leadership in Jamaica and the vast majority of post-colonial Caribbean nations. I would perhaps demand somewhat more of the first bold quote from Peter Drucker from the perspective that economic and social development, above all, not only *means* management but truly *requires* management. Looked at in this manner, the second bold quote becomes much more inextricably sequential. It therefore becomes obvious that there is no effective leadership without effective management. As a rule, we have substituted political ideology for sound management, compromised, if not marginalized, the focus and ability of the technocracy and generally ensured that government decisions are seldom made with due attention to rational deliberation of facts in keeping with the reality of our circumstances.

In a very welcome exchange with a friend, Lloyd Stanford, he commented on my conviction that the two-party-system-democracy model is problematic at best and deficient at worst in its ability to address far too many of the critical issues facing countries like Jamaica. His very intriguing observations are reproduced below:

> *Here is an* **iconoclastic** *comment ....*
> *I think you are focusing on the* **wrong aspect of statecraft***: well managed countries are not run by political parties but by a political 'executive' that 'steer' a well- oiled administrative apparatus, itself run by* **responsible** *public servants with a sense of the public interest. You must look at Etzioni's* **Bureaucracy and Democracy** *and consider the theses of people like Courtney Blackman re 'economic* **management'***.*
>
> *The exercise of 'political rationality'- a kind of pragmatism by the shrewdest leaders who usually abandon ideology when actually in power - tempered by 'technocratic' rationality often leads to good governance. It probably explains why there are some amazing stretches of successful government by unlikely 'administrations'. Perhaps in Jamaica's case we have had a lot of bad management because we did not maintain the balance.*

The really bad example of politicians trying to run a country is Haiti, and almost every bad development I have noticed in Jamaica, including the extraordinary presence of slums all over remind me of the awful developments I began to notice there from 1954.

I don't think it matters whether you have two parties, one or 12: the key is how you actually run the country. You just must have **'capacity'***.*

There is much that is worth pondering here, not the least of which is the view that the number of competing political parties is of no significance. Also noteworthy is the idea that a blend of political and technocratic rationality *often leads to good governance.*

In the first case, a multiplicity of competing parties does matter if for no other reason than that, almost inevitably, the eventual government ends up being a motley group of power seekers that arrives at a majority through convenient but highly unstable compromise. Most often, these arrangements of convenience, if they survive, achieve very little as the minority that assured a majority is more committed to securing its own influence than in achieving the policy objectives of the larger group in the coalition. Also, cohesiveness and performance deteriorate as the number of parties in the coalition increases. Leadership by its very nature is more effective when it is concentrated rather than dispersed as is more often than not the case with coalitions of convenience. Successive governments of Italy exemplify the dilemma. This is definitely not a preferred model.

In the second case, we are hoping for Utopia. The evidence indicates that the civil service in Third World nations is nearly always politicized. This is, of course, part of the matrix of political manipulation and patronage that ensures the precedence of political ideology over sound policy and reliable measurement of performance as the primary directive device. In Jamaica, for example, it is now not unusual to witness the re-assignment or undermining of senior civil servants, including permanent secretaries, when a new administration takes office. This is perhaps one of the most destructive departures from the heritage of the colonial era and affects the technocracy in two significant ways. The first is a decline in administrative effective-ness; the second is the migration of the most competent technocrats into the private sector. Sadly, even politicians out of power think and behave as if they know every-thing; they seldom listen to or take advice, are very willing to speak much more than they are to listen and appear to have a proclivity for misleading their constituents and the public in general purely out of unabashed self-interest. In either case, the *capacity* that my friend correctly sees as necessary disappears from the point of most critical need at a time when this can least be afforded.

The Orane address as well as the **World Bank Report** confirms the steady decline in our good fortune following the halcyon days immediately following Independence. Still, if this is not convincing enough let us observe commentary from Martin Henry, contributor to the Sunday, August 5, 2012 issue of **The Gleaner** during the celebrations of **Jamaica 50.** Henry points out that:

> ......***our country has sustained a stable and functional parlia-mentary democracy, which is not exactly a minor achievement in the postcolonial world.*** *But this has not been without the blot of garrisons, political tribalism, and political violence which has cost the lives of tens of thousands of citizens, directly or indirectly, has internally displaced multiple thousands more and hampered development.*

> *We should, at the Grand Gala tomorrow, observe a minute's silence for the thousands dead from our nation's Independence politics. We have closed 50 years of Independence with a comparatively robust democracy and a great deal of personal freedom as a people.*

> *A very important out-turn of the first 50 years is the reduction in the rate of population growth and reduction in the fertility rate. Migration has assisted mightily in keeping our numbers down within manage-able limits, but not without the loss of the majority of citizens who have acquired tertiary education, an outflow now running at some 85 per cent.*

A significant failure is that the Jamaican economy has never been able to absorb the majority of its trained people.

It is now the done thing to place economic management and economic performance at the top of the agenda. **But even more vital and basic in a sovereign state is the security of its people, the protection of their rights and freedoms, and the delivery of justice to them.** *On these core axes of assessment, governance in independent Jamaica has been a miserable failure. In 50 years Jamaica has earned the unenviable distinction of being among the top three countries for its murder rate, moving from about four per 100,000 in 1962 to nearly 60 per 100,000.*

The optimism of the first decade was accompanied by a growing sense of inequality, and a sense that the benefits of growth were not being experienced by the urban poor. This, combined with the effects of a slowdown in the global economy in 1970, prompted the electorate to change government, electing the PNP (People's National Party) in 1972. *Despite efforts to create more socially equitable policies in education and health, Jamaica continued to lag economically, with its gross national product having fallen in 1980 to some 25% below the 1972 level.*

Rising foreign and local debt, accompanied by large fiscal deficits, resulted in the invitation of the International Monetary Fund (IMF) financing from the United States and others, and the imposition of IMF austerity measures (with a greater than 25% interest rate per year).

I have made bold, points of reference that are of particular importance as we attempt to understand and appreciate the reasons for the very reasonable contention that the two-party-system-democracy is not necessarily a satisfactory system of governance, especially when conditions deteriorate noticeably on a national scale. It should be noted that the beginning of the decline in Jamaica's performance is coincident with the slowdown in the global economy and the subsequent change in government from the JLP to the PNP. It is very convenient to conclude on this account that the conservative nature of the JLP government was advantageous while the more socialistic tendency of the PNP was harmful. This would be a misguided conclusion in my view, mainly because of the overwhelming evidence provided by the subsequent years of interchanging government regimes in which neither party fared better than the other in terms of what was accomplished. In addition, the last highlighted section of the excerpt above very clearly indicates that dark clouds were beginning to gather during the early years alongside fairly robust economic growth. It is also striking that Jamaica was not unique in its experience with economic difficulties at the time. As notable perhaps is the difference in approach to these difficulties from one former colony to another.

Consider Barbados, for example. The **World Bank Report** reveals that:

> *[Barbados] was faster and more successful than other Caribbean countries in its diversification strategy. This in part can be explained by the early government action. Da Costa (2007) also points to Barbados' smaller and less efficient sugar production units and its favorable investment climate as factors in this success.*

> *- From 1940, the country had a tradition of pursuing medium-term plans. The approach towards development planning has been largely "indicative," with the government providing the institutional and policy framework and the environment for the private sector to provide the stimulus for economic activity.*

> *- In the pre-independence period, Barbados maintained balanced budgets or small deficits, and unlike other Caribbean colonies, it did not rely on annual grants from the United Kingdom. This well organized fiscal policy*

made it possible for the country to use early incentives to promote FDI.
[Foreign Development Incentive]

- Since the first election, large investments in human capital forged a well-
educated workforce, giving Barbados a literacy rate of 83 percent at the
time of the independence, the region's highest. Free secondary education
was introduced by 1962, and the country's outlays on public health are
relatively high at around 18 percent of total expenditures.

Barbados is held in very high regard internationally. The former United Nations Secretary General, Kofi Annan, is quoted on **PRWeb.com** as saying that: *"Barbados consistently punches above its weight."* This status is also reflected in Barbados being regarded as a middle-high income country, with annual per capita income at around US $24,000.00. Significantly, Barbados is ranked 47th out of nearly 200 countries, on the **UNDP's Human Development Index** and has a life expectancy at birth of 77 years. Jamaica is ranked 80th and has a life expectancy of 73 years. Does this invalidate the argument about the inadequacy of the two-party-system-democracy? Not at all. The regrettable reality is that Barbados is the exception and not the rule. Unfortunately, this may not remain the case for very long as Barbados has some dark clouds approaching over the horizon.

Despite this rosy picture of Barbados, we should be aware that its debt/GDP ratio of 117% may be reasonable cause for some apprehension. This is not baseless given the current universal disquiet about national deficits and what they portend for the future economic viability of nations experiencing excessively unfavorable debt/GDP ratios. In the case of Jamaica the ratio is 139%. This has given rise to a sky-is-falling anxiety among international as well as local financial institutions and experts. This appears to engender excessive political timidity rather than bold action in response to the worrisome problem. It may or may not be of some comfort to realize that Japan, clearly a highly respected first world economy, has a debt/GDP ratio of 230%. The distressing reality behind the Jamaica deficit is the fact that Jamaica does not have the substantial underpinnings or history of a resilient economy that could inspire either international or local institutional confidence in its capacity to deal urgently or positively with its economic problems. In short, as a nation, we have not only consistently failed to live up to our potential but have recklessly created and nurtured our own stumbling blocks. Perhaps the most lethal of these is the relentless scourge of crime and corruption.

In general, I do subscribe to the theory that people deserve the government they elect. However, it does not necessarily follow that there is never or should never be the chance that the people's choice could surprise us favorably. So tragic has been our misfortune that we have never been pleasantly surprised by any of our successive governments since Independence. Even luck evades us. It may be true that we make our own luck. If this is indeed the case, we have a great deal to do.

c. Performance & Accountability

Performance against clear goals and objectives has never been a secure point of reference in our traditional political landscape. Instead, posturing is much preferred by the leadership class. Indifference or resignation is the common preference of the vast majority of citizens. In either case little preparation or effort is required as these conditions appear to be hereditary. As a result accountability is very seldom of serious concern in spite of the fact that performance and accountability are opposite sides of the same coin. The gross indifference to this relationship lies at the very heart of our endless dilemma.

Latterly, it is generally the case that Jamaican political leaders do not lead. Rather, they make adjustments to the constantly changing nature of their political and social environment. This matches up perfectly with the now engrained principle of accommodation and adjustment by the general population. One may wonder which came first, the security blanket of adjustment by politicians or the comfortable accommodation by constituents. This, however, does not contribute in any useful way to our understanding of the situation or to our attempt to provide likely solutions. Both conditions and their unfavorable impact on Jamaican society are effectively documented by Obika Gray as well as by Carl Stone in his work, **Class, State, and Democracy in Jamaica.** While undoubtedly complex and confusing, the meandering but twin stream flow of political affiliation in Jamaica makes party affiliation almost congenital. This observation does not apply uniquely to Jamaica or most Third World countries. The condition is noticeable in First World countries as well. The critical difference between these contrived Worlds lies in the willingness of the latter to question performance and demand accountability. This variation has great value because it often elicits acknowledgement of failure and sometimes adjustment in the approach of political leadership to important issues. In this respect there is great potential for politically unfavorable consequences if either performance or accountability is ignored by political leaders.

It should be evident that in order to even contemplate performance in any meaningful way we must agree on goals or objectives. Almost simultaneously we have to agree as well on the standards against which performance will be measured. Douglas Orane demonstrated this necessary link indelibly in his portrayal of his company, GraceKennedy, as it went about living its vision, setting and meeting its goals and objectives and satisfying the needs and expectations of its customers, employees and shareholders. Clearly, the subsequent success of GraceKennedy is not accidental. The great news in all this is the fact that such remarkable progress is not limited to private enterprise. As a nation, especially a relatively small one, it is entirely possible that we could emulate the GraceKennedy model with similar results. This, after all, is the implication of Orane's extensive revelation of the model.

Consider the very straightforward plan that resulted in the enviable achievements of Orane's company over the last couple of decades: embrace acceptable and useful values, determine a company vision, set goals and objectives, measure performance against these, share success with all stakeholders, learn from others. The excerpt below from Orane's address clearly reveals the outcome from this disciplined and enlightened approach:

> *GraceKennedy was listed on the Jamaica Stock Exchange in 1986. Its annual sales were then US$167 million and the equity of the firm was*

US$22 million. Fast forward 25 years and our sales in 2011 were US$ 677 million an increase of 305%, and the equity of the company at the end of December 2011 was US$339 million, an increase of 1440%. This track record of creating prosperity has been achieved by firstly having a clear set of values — honesty, integrity and trust. Secondly, developing a culture of inclusiveness which is both egalitarian and meritocratic. As an example GraceKennedy has offered purchases of shares to our employees since 1925, three years after the company was founded in 1922. Consequently, we all look at GraceKennedy as our own company to build. We have several hundreds of our employees and pensioners who are shareholders today.

We have encouraged the training, development, coaching and mentorship of our people at every level so that their aspirations can be achieved within the company without having to leave and seek opportunities elsewhere. This has created what I call a culture of intrapreneurship [sic] which allows us to be creative in our development of new products and services, while at the same time absorbing innovations from wherever they may emerge in our global environment.

The real wonder of this example is that the methodology and process are as free as the air we breathe and extremely promising of success. Anyone may legitimately ask, why then is it that such an example has never been quickly adopted and aggressively pursued by even a single government regime over fifty years? The reason is frighteningly simple: There is no credible demand for performance against clearly stated and publicly acknowledged objectives or goals. Neither is there any attendant requirement of accountability in our two-party-system-democracy. In the absence of any tradition of performance and accountability there is no reason for political leaders to contemplate unfavorable consequences.

In my estimation, this feature of our politics, more than anything else, guarantees the perpetuation of incompetence and mismanagement and, ultimately, failure. This amounts to a bewildering paradox when we consider the insistent claim that we are among the freest people on earth and enjoy the coveted freedom to choose those who govern at prescribed intervals. I can imagine nothing more harmful to our personal and national wellbeing than our demonstrated willingness to constantly devalue our freedom by accepting a *status quo* that consistently offers nothing more than questionable, unfulfilled promises. Some understandably see this quandary as hope when in reality it is merely symptomatic of our willingness to adjust, accommodate, accept and endure.

We need to be reminded constantly that the *status quo* is seldom our friend. It tends to lure us into a highly questionable state of comfort when a state of discomfort is much more promising of a more satisfactory future. We will surely become more sensitive to this contention when we come to contemplate alternatives to the *status quo*.

d. The First Female Prime Minister

Gender breakers of the leadership tradition in historically patriarchal societies have become much less surprising. To a very great extent this is primarily because of the increased frequency of the occurrence and the relatively large numbers of readily available examples. In 2013 there were seventeen countries that have female political leaders: from Australia's Julia Gillard to Germany's Angela Merkel to Liberia's Johnson-Sirleaf to Trinidad and Tobago's Persad-Bissessar. Generally, the major surprise of their rise now seems to be more as examples of what is possible in societies that were traditionally patriarchal than as indicators that gender swaps in and of themselves necessarily signal inevitable improvement in the quality of leadership or in the execution of leadership responsibilities. In this sense they are much more meaningful as change markers than as change makers. Their arrival at the very pinnacle of political power is no longer automatically transformative in consequence. This appears to be most certainly the reality in the case of Jamaica and the main reason for making the occurrence worthy of particular reference here.

Many Jamaicans see the 2006 election of Portia Lucretia Simpson-Miller as the first female Prime Minister as a real game changer in Jamaican politics although her initial term as Prime Minister was less than two years. She

regained the position in January of 2012. Like the majority of remarkably successful Jamaicans, she overcame the most challenging of personal circumstances
to achieve success. On both a personal as well as national level her recognition by
Time Magazine as one of the one hundred most influential women in the world
in 2012 is significant. Simpson-Miller had been a PNP stalwart from her earliest
teenage years. Of great value to party supporters and party power brokers is her
loyalty and diligence over 40 years on her way up the party ladder from the early
1970's when she served in local government through her later years as a Member
of Parliament and cabinet minister. She is regarded as among the strongest, most
focused voices on behalf of the poor and the young in today's Jamaica.

In spite of all this, however, Simpson-Miller has almost as many detractors as she
has supporters regarding her capacity as a leader. This difficulty is made worse by the
fact that this is as much the case even within her own political party and cabinet. In her
defense, Jamaica is now more than ever a very class-sensitive society in which class status is as weightily influenced by shade of complexion as by education or intellectual heft.
The influence of the former has diminished admirably over time while the influence of
the latter now appears to be dominant. It is very difficult to discern the extent to which
the Prime Minister's predicament may be due more to the actual lack of significant
scholastic achievement than to the still meaningful relevance of skin shade.

It is very noteworthy that the question of gender does not dominate the debate
thus supporting the earlier point concerning gender breakers. In general, this question of leadership capacity has attained a permanency that not only lends it credibility but actually makes it more difficult for the Prime Minister to accomplish any
of her more difficult and politically controversial but necessary objectives. Among
these, of course, is coming to an agreement with the IMF on the matter of financial
support for Jamaica's ailing economy. Sharp criticism by party members substantiates the problem. For example, Errol Ennis, a member of the earlier Patterson
PNP government recently stated in the Gleaner that:

> "One year after a new administration, this status quo is intact. This results
> in alarming inertias ...... due to incompatibility of political intent and

administrative inertia........it is urgent that leadership within the admin-
istration find the wherewithal to enable the state machinery to operate in
a manner that ensures the welfare of our people".

In addition, it is well documented in the local press as well as acknowledged anecdotally among keen observers of local politics that there is enduring rancor between the two main factions within the PNP: the one supporting Minister of Finance, Peter Phillips, and the other steadfastly committed to Prime Minister, Simpson-Miller. Not surprisingly, Phillips had opposed Simpson-Miller in elections for the leadership of the PNP.

Notwithstanding her troubles, Simpson-Miller remains the darling of the poor and generally marginalized segment of the voting population that in the nature of things comprises the majority of active voters. In typically biting political irony, it is not unusual to hear detractors say that Simpson-Miller so adores the poor that she creates as many as she can in her own constituency. Simpson-Miller's constituency happens to be among the very poorest in the country and has been so for the four decades that she has been its representative. It appears that this block of voters has concluded that since their condition has steadfastly remained unchanged regardless of the changes in political leadership, nothing is lost in constantly supporting one from among them. In fact, it is quite understandable that such a choice could be seen by this relatively monolithic group as more reasonably hopeful than any other. This theory is very clearly supported by the fact that in the last national elections in 2011 Simpson-Miller received nearly 95% of the votes cast in her constituency.

All things considered, Simpson-Miller does not appear generally to be any less effective than the overwhelming majority of her male predecessors if we judge effectiveness on the basis of outcomes versus expectations. After all it is extremely difficult to argue convincingly that more than one or two of her male counterparts achieved significant, sustainable or sustained positive change in Jamaica's economy, regardless of whether this is viewed from a purely fiscal, productivity or human welfare perspective. There is no convincing evidence to the contrary over these past fifty years. Our failures and decline have been steady and unresponsive to our political attempts to address them. In the meantime, we have undergone welcome change in our national status, endured alternating political parties and governments, embraced gender change at the level of head of government surprisingly early and flirted with youthful, exuberant leadership. None of these has meaningfully improved our fortunes.

It may be considered willfully negligent not to ask why it is that none of the foregoing events has brought discernible positive change in our circumstances or engendered greater hopefulness in how the broad cross section of our people sees our future. The answer to this question should not surprise anyone since the question represents a variation on a common theme: why are we stagnant or in reverse in all the critical aspects of nation building? The answer is as lacking in surprise as it is invariable: the *status quo* lives. It lives a secure, protected life while performance and accountability remain unattractive instruments of nation building that may be constantly ignored without penalty.

The lesson here is clear: we must find a different, more effective way in which to address our intractable problems.

e. The Matter of Becoming a Republic

In better times we could justify making this feel-good political maneuver a priority. It is very difficult to imagine a worse time in which to contemplate, let alone actually implement, such an expensive indulgence. There are a few interesting aspects that we may wish to consider.

In a March 2012 article by Nick Davis for **BBC News,** *Jamaica Debates Republic Option,* a survey reveals some quite surprising results: 60% of those canvassed believed Jamaica would be better off today if it had remained a British colony, against 16% that thought they would be worse off. Even so, this does not necessarily mean that all those who see republic status unfavorably would vote against the proposition; after all this is a poll, not a vote in an election. A similar survey was done in a number of former colonies in Central and Southern Africa during the early to mid-nineteen nineties. The outcome mirrored the Jamaica results. One may reasonably assume that there are good reasons for the surprising results, especially when these are from disparate countries. Not the least of these has to be the reality that as bad as we may think colonization was, the anticipated benefits from achieving independence have never been realized. Worse, most now believe that they never will be or can be.

Undoubtedly, there is a powerful, politically prideful attraction to being totally severed from our former colonial masters that could trump the misgivings clearly indicated by the surveys in question. There is also the matter of cost, however. In the same Davis article, Jamaica's Merrick Needham, a Jamaican etiquette and protocol expert, points out that "..... *it'll cost millions and millions of Jamaican dollars... think about what can be done in terms of healthcare, security, crime reduction with that money".* In addition, there are associated inconveniences such as visa requirements and the loss of other, sometimes useful, preferential arrangements occasioned by being a member of the still active and admired Commonwealth Club. In the final analysis it comes down to the matter of priority. Indications are that this is not the time.

Ironically, among the aggressive supporters of Jamaica becoming a republic is former Prime Minister, Percival Patterson. The surprise here is that Patterson uniquely occupied the position of Prime Minister for four unbroken terms but never made attaining the status of a republic a priority. Another former Prime Minister from the opposition party, Bruce Golding, is also a very enthusiastic proponent of republican status as is the current Prime Minister, of course. Certainly, on this issue there seems to be unusual political consensus. Still, given the parlous state of Jamaica's finances it is inconceivable that the incumbent Prime Minister would act on her inclination. Another quote from the Nick Davis commentary emphasizes the point: *But with Jamaica battling with high unemployment and a debt burden that is 130% of GDP at nearly $18bn, some wonder if becoming a republic should be a priority.* If only reason and politics could be not simply strange but friendly bedfellows!

Of course, there are countries in the region like Guyana, Trinidad & Tobago and Haiti that are republics. There is no trustworthy evidence that their subsequent complete separation from their colonial masters has brought them practical, noteworthy incremental benefits. At the same time I do not deny the value of the nationally meaningful psychological comfort that could possibly come from becoming a republic. Nevertheless, one must wonder, for practical purposes, just how much freer a nation can be than being independent. The unsettled question remains whether this desire is worth the effort and cost in its fulfillment at a time when a number of survival issues should justifiably take precedence. In this vein one cannot ignore the very passionate and defensible argument of Patrick Robinson, the esteemed Jamaican judge and president of the International Criminal Tribunal for the former Yugoslavia in The Hague, Netherlands. In his June 19, 2012 address at the University of London: **The Monarchy, Republicanism and the Privy Council:** *The Enduring Cry for Freedom,* Robinson makes an impressive case in support of his expressed preference.

Like Robinson, I despise all monarchies and for identical reasons. In his words:

> *A monarchical system of government is inherently undemocratic, since the will of the people has no influence on the process by which the Monarch, as Head of State, is appointed. …….there is another reason why the present monarchical system is inappropriate for Jamaica: Jamaica is a post-oppression society and its people should not be asked to have as its Head of State a person who symbolizes the oppression inflicted on their enslaved and other ancestors. By far the worst relic of enslavement, indentureship and colonialism is that they have left Jamaicans with a muddled sense of their identity. Colonisation has left ingrained in the psyche of Jamaicans the feeling that they are not good enough, that what they look like is not good enough and that what is foreign, especially if it is white, English, European or American is better.*

I understand the sense of disgust that is so very palpably expressed here. At the same time, and more fundamentally, one must marvel at the fact that as a people we embraced and still today accept without question after more than 300 years, the very two-party-system-democracy that enshrines the monarchy. It seems strange that we now adamantly wish to reject our monarch as the head of state. Logically, can we question the legitimacy of the monarchy and not question the legitimacy of its progeny or antecedent (depending on one's point of view), the two-party-system-democracy that was similarly inherited? It is quite a challenge not to see the system and the monarchy as a tie-in contract. This is not a question of meagre significance. It is one that we must constantly bear in mind as we continue on our quest for reasonable alternatives to our traditional system of governance.

I also disagree fervently that, according to Robinson, Jamaicans have a *muddled sense of identity*. I can think of no other survivors of British subjugation in the Caribbean or elsewhere that are as certain of their identity as Jamaicans. This is especially the case among those in the Diaspora where one should reasonably expect this psychological deficiency to be most evident. My contention is supported by an excerpt from the October 9, 2012 article, **Jamaica Profile** in **BBC News** *Latin America & the Caribbean*. The excerpt states: *Known for its strong sense of self identity expressed through its music, food and rich cultural mix, Jamaica's influence extends far beyond its shores.*

Quite surprisingly, Robinson makes the case against his own argument remarkably early in his address when he boasts: *After all, there is a cachet attached to being Jamaican that goes far beyond the running track. It is not every country that can claim that its name has given birth to a new word in the English language. If you are not already privy to it, let me tell you that in the next edition of any reputable English dictionary you will see the word, "jamaicanly adv. defying the odds with style, flair and aplomb in such a manner as would normally be deemed incredible or impossible".*

On the one hand, this denies the urgency of the need to dispose of the monarchical system; on the other it clearly overwhelms the argument justifying the validity of the claim that republican status is an historical and psychological necessity.

4

INTERSECTION OR MAJOR
TRAFFIC CIRCLE?

a. Recognizing The Difference

The increasingly productivity-robbing and emotionally taxing traffic congestion on the roadways all over the city of Kingston and lower St. Andrew is symptomatic of the political, social and economic strangulation we face in our national
life. In a manner of speaking, we are expending untold amounts of energy constantly crawling around, falling into potholes, being bruised and bloodied, getting
out of potholes only to fall into wider and deeper potholes. Obviously, if we are
continually in potholes or always have to navigate potholes, it is extremely difficult
to detect the road ahead. Under such conditions how do we tell whether we are
at a simple intersection or a major traffic circle? This analogy helps to explain our
inability or unwillingness to recognize not only where we are but more importantly where we are headed.

In truth, it really is not as impossible as it may appear to recognize the
essential nature of our whereabouts. After all, if we keep falling into the same
potholes time and time again we inevitably come to understand that we are
in fact traversing the same area of ground and in effect getting nowhere. By

simple deduction we come to realize that we have been traveling in a circle. By dint of our own activity we have managed to widen this circle to a size so large that the vast majority of us are disoriented or unable to exit the circle. The few that manage to exit have no certain knowledge of the exit they have taken. Now we must choose whether to continue as we are accustomed or do something different. We should slow down, stop and take in the lay of the land, consult with fellow travelers and agree on how we should proceed. We wish with all our hearts that we were in fact at a simple intersection. Alas, we are not and the reality will remain quite indifferent to our wishes. Try as we may we cannot turn the traffic circle or roundabout into a simple intersection. We have decisions to make.

Unlike a major traffic circle, a simple intersection offers relatively few options. A major traffic circle exists as a means to safely and effectively slow traffic while allowing reasonably steady flow, especially where multiple roads feed into and emanate from the circle. Naturally, such a traffic circle offers a number of options. No one really needs to explain the quandary here as it is common knowledge that very few drivers in Jamaica follow the rules governing traffic, whether on a circle or a straightaway. In fact, some drivers even purposely proceed around the circle in the wrong direction on the assumption, or perhaps the hope, that such a deliberately contrarian approach will bring better and faster results. Not surprisingly, this only serves to exacerbate the problem. A common consequence, of course, is that we have many severe accidents.

It seems entirely probable that under these conditions the situation will become so dire that the circle may need to be converted to a triage station before we may be able to address the problem to good effect. Such is the state of our national life in Jamaica. Regardless of this state of affairs there is some advantage in knowing where we are, however. At least we can now glance back from whence we came and look forward to where we wish to be. It is all but inconceivable that we will not learn important and helpful lessons from this perspective.

b. Who Decides Progress?

There should be very little confusion or controversy regarding either where we are coming from or where we are. These are clearly *faits accomplis* and largely problematic only in retrospect. More to the point is who will decide the speed, manner and direction in which we proceed from where we are. If the consideration frightens us, it should. We have not given sufficient thought to the significance and urgency of the question. Had we done so we would long ago have questioned our civic behaviors with much more determination and vigor and demanded with much greater insistence that our leaders perform against their commitments, fully aware of their accountability. As citizens we have certainly not been as persistent as we need to be in our opposition to the *status quo*.

We appear to have decided that our personal responsibility for the running of our country ends once we have elected our political leaders. Our political leaders seem to have decided that their own responsibility ends once they are elected to office. This is not stalemate. This is stagnation and reversal. As citizens we are now complicit in what has become a pathological condition whose most obvious symptom is extensive accommodation of the *status quo*. In other words, it has become a national pastime not to rock the boat. Yet, managing our country, any country for that matter, is of necessity a cooperative yet rocky affair. If the sea of state is always calm there is every likelihood that not much of significance is being accomplished. While hierarchy is tolerated and often necessary, it is insufficient as an instrument of management. The constant engagement of the citizenry is essentially what makes national management effective and leadership trustworthy.

As citizens we therefore play decisive roles in our country's performance, its successes as well as its failures. We fail in our roles if we remain uninformed, uneducated or undereducated, disengaged, indifferent or resigned. Whether by default or purposeful action, after all is said and done, we are the major deciders of our progress. We may claim otherwise as much as we want but neither our obligation nor culpability will disappear. Pointing the finger of blame or guilt at the sly, slippery politicians we elect is an exercise in futility that reminds me of the truism that when we point a finger every other finger points directly back at us.

c. Obligation to The People vs. Commitment to The *Status Quo*

Politicians start out with the very best of intentions then lose their way for reasons far too numerous and varied for us to speculate about here. It remains generally true, however, that there is a migration of focus from the acknowledged needs of their constituents to their own personal and professional ambitions. Quite often this leads to shortcomings that range from inaction to malfeasance. In any event, politicians very soon after winning office cease to recognize the continued existence of their primary obligation – the unquestionable responsibility to attend to, and hopefully, satisfy the needs of those who elected them. This failing is so commonplace that the people, more often than not, lower their expectations to meet the level of substandard performance on the part of their government. And so we end up with unmet obligations and not even a veiled threat of retribution from the general population that must endure the unfavorable consequences.

Needless to say, this is more cooperation by default rather than cooperation by design. Of course, the consequences are not mitigated by this circumstance. Among the most harmful and pervasive of outcomes, of course, is the continued security of the *status quo*. Ironically, change, which at this time is more necessary than ever, is now least likely to occur. And so the *status quo* remains in safe harbor, the economy falters, the welfare of the people is neglected and progress is stymied in an endless cycle. This long history of accommodation has become collective acquiescence. As a result, this dilemma is not seen as the intractable, debilitating problem that it truly is. Instead, it is accepted as par for the course as we adjust our expectations to accommodate the inevitably unfavorable consequences. You may recall the story of the experiment with the frog in the boiling water and the sad but highly instructive outcome.

It remains exceedingly difficult to believe that the entire leadership class consciously and constantly ignores the combination of economic stagnation and collective hardships. There is no doubt that both are nurtured by the *status quo* even in the midst of acknowledged and frequently discussed lack of performance and indifference to accountability. As alarming as such purposeful indifference to our circumstances would be, if this were in fact the case, any remedy could be much more easily and very directly applied. The application of any remedy becomes that much more challenging when the malady is so deeply entrenched in the very fabric of national life that it seems as natural as the sea shore and just as undemanding of our direct and constant attention. In this manner the commitment to the *status quo* has become a natural condition that is at the core of the clutch of problems we face.

Our chances of success as a nation would be very greatly advanced were the obligation of the leadership class to the people as natural a reality as is this apparent commitment to the *status quo*, whether by intention or by default. Hopefully, just as is the case with the sea shore, natural disasters have a way of rearranging the landscape, redirecting our attention as well as resetting our priorities. Our clutch of problems is the squall that precedes the category five hurricanes we will surely experience if we continue to fail to appreciate the seriousness of our dilemma and the implications of our protracted reluctance to address its basic causes with fore-sight and fortitude.

PART TWO

MOVING AHEAD

Life exacts a price from us all, without exception. It is called living.

5

VISION 2030 JAMAICA

There can be no doubt that **Vision 2030 Jamaica** substantiates the fact that there is unquestionable recognition, certainly among the leadership class, that action must be initiated to move the country ahead after decades of stagnation or reversal on every critical front. While it is true that a nation never really dies, a nation may become so dysfunctional that figuratively speaking, death may be seen by some as an option worthy of consideration. Of grave concern are the obvious and pervasive decline in civility, the alarming extent of indiscipline and lawlessness and the rampant, unthinking defensiveness by so many Jamaicans of the generally worrisome state of affairs. This depressing combination, along with the periodic but constant exodus of members of the entrepreneurial and professional classes, must leave the concerned observer with a sense of doom that cannot be ignored or easily appeased. Sadly, the unyielding intensity of all this does enhance the self-fulfilling potential of this sense of doom.

To the extent that these insults to national well-being stimulate the concerns, fears, hopes and insights that must surely underlie **Vision 2030 Jamaica,** one must remain encouraged that paradise, though constantly elusory, is not yet permanently lost. It is from such a perspective that we should view this attempt to right our floundering ship of state and secure the implied promise of the tradition of sacrifice evident in the remarkable contributions of our forefathers, a number of whom we so proudly remember and honor with much pomp and ceremony at every Independence anniversary.

a. Objective

As national plans go, **Vision 2030 Jamaica** is most ambitious and impressive in its scope and longer-term intent as well as exemplary in the manner of its presentation to those whose support it most certainly will need in order to succeed in the long term – the ordinary citizen. The selling of the plan is driven by a series of measured videos by plan categories, a simple summary of the plan, an executive summary of the plan and, of course, the exhaustive 400-page complete plan document. There is a clear statement of vision, explicit national goals, stated anticipated outcomes and extensive strategies for accomplishing the plan's objectives. Not surprisingly, all outcomes to date are adequately graphed, benchmarks abound and performance graphically evaluated against both benchmarks and targets. It is encouraging that there is a commitment to review the plan every three years.

Very clearly, stated or not, the framers of the plan appear not only to recognize the dilemma that Jamaica faces but accept in principle that the longer we delay attacking our problems the more we continue to degrade our ability to address them effectively and in a timely manner. The plan is unique in the history of national planning, demands unusual commitment and sacrifice and sets in place very challenging standards of achievement by which Jamaica may be judged over the next several years. In my view, it demonstrates a shift toward a different approach to addressing problems that have plagued us with snowballing consequences since Independence. Above all, the plan seems to recognize the constricting effects of the *status quo*. I will incorporate this plan into the radical approach I intend to suggest and that I am convinced is vitally necessary for our survival as a viable, exemplary nation.

There is no reason why this national plan should not be read and studied, at least in the form of the executive summary, by all who may have or hope to have contributions to make to our progress or may simply have the best interest of Jamaica at heart. The plan is surely worthy of our commitment and ongoing attention. Acknowledged or not, every citizen, unavoidably, has a vested interest in this project which is nothing short of what is claimed by its framers: *Vision 2030 Jamaica - National Development Plan is the 'roadmap' for making "Jamaica, the place of choice to live, work, raise families and do business".*

At the very outset let us agree that there is no need to quibble over what this implies in terms of objective. What we are obliged to do is to understand and appreciate what resources will be necessary in any attempt to support this vision. Neither should the reality escape us that as impressive a roadmap as **Vision 2030 Jamaica** may be, it has relevance, currency and effectiveness only to the extent that it recognizes that the topography it now reflects will continue to change incessantly, with scant regard for any particular roadmap. This does mean that our ability to respond to such changes is integral to the pace at which we succeed or whether we succeed at all.

Although the details of the project are exceptionally easy to access on line and elsewhere, I feel compelled to present its four stated goals here:

1. **Jamaicans Are Empowered To Achieve Their Fullest Potential.**
2. **Jamaican Society Is Secure, Cohesive And Just.**
3. **Jamaica's Economy Is Prosperous.**
4. **Jamaica Has A Healthy National Environment.**

Notably, there are 15 stated national outcomes and 84 national strategies that accompany these goals. In the final analysis, however, the plan's success is totally at the mercy of how effectively it is implemented, monitored and progress evaluated. In this case the devil is not in the details as is often claimed when we are faced with complex issues. Here, the real devil is truly in the implementation. The details are elegantly in place, and, traditionally, we are not without significant ability to monitor and evaluate. In fact, most Third World countries could be seen as being fairly gifted or competent in these respects. In addition, there is never a shortage of external third party monitoring and evaluating of national plans such as this whether these assists are solicited or not. Still, there are serious challenges to be faced.

b. Challenges

Our real, definitive, inescapable challenge lies in our ability to implement. We have never been good at this. Once again, our overwhelming reluctance to attack the *status quo* is directly relevant.

Obviously, we have had many a plan that is similar to, though not as ambitious as, **Vision 2030 Jamaica**. In fact, Jamaica has had a fairly long history of development planning, the most recent prior to **Vision 2030 Jamaica** being for the period 1990-1995. In addition, there has been what **Vision 2030 Jamaica** identifies as *development planning exercises* such as the National Industrial Policy (NIP) for 1996-2001. There is no evidence that any of these plans or exercises was successfully implemented. This is a bleak history against which to anticipate that this time the outcome will be different. Perhaps this time will be different in spite of the history because the stakes have never been as high. This time the cost of failure is likely to be significantly higher than was the cost of failure for any previous national plan. Unfortunately, cumulative failures in pursuit of related ventures tend to increase the cost of the latest attempt dramatically. This time the attempt has to be different if we are to succeed.

There is another worry. Unavoidably, there are significant costs associated with the implementation of **Vision 2030 Jamaica**. These costs have not been quantified and itemized although indicated as included in the budgets of the particularly affected government ministries. Given acknowledged scarce resources and the known history of inefficiency of these ministries, one must wonder whether this allocation is not a recipe for failure. While this is obviously the most convenient way to allocate and manage the funding of **Vision 2030 Jamaica** it is just as obviously the most likely to be altogether ineffective or stymied. It is difficult to imagine that any ministry will willingly sacrifice a minister's immediate-term priorities for the longer-term priorities of **Vision 2030 Jamaica**. This is perhaps the most worrisome challenge of all since we know that whoever controls the purse determines priorities and by extension outcomes as well. In short, he who pays the piper calls the tune. The funding for **Vision 2030 Jamaica** should be clearly identified, itemized and isolated and not managed by individual ministries or ministers of government.

i. Scope - Priorities - Resources

The scope of **Vision 2030 Jamaica** is virtually all encompassing. It touches on all the critically significant aspects of national life, from agriculture, crime and education to the environment, security and tourism. There is no doubt that all these things are in need of attention. There is more than reasonable doubt, however, that they all can be attended to simultaneously or to the same extent, especially if we recognize that there are very limited resources available in terms of both management capacity and finances. In keeping with this concern, consider this reality: about 55% of government spending goes towards paying the nation's debt, while 25% goes to paying wages. This leaves just 20% for everything else - including education, security and health. As virtuous as our intentions may be, we cannot escape the fact that we are resource poor. A common saying among Jamaicans explains the dilemma very well: *we have to cut our suit to fit the cloth we have*. The question then is how best to determine our priorities.

Crime & Corruption:

It is generally known and readily acknowledged that crime and corruption together comprise the single most critical and destabilizing scourge affecting the present and future wellbeing of Jamaica. No one can convincingly minimize the pervasive nature of this devastating combination. On this basis alone this duo has to be addressed as the number one priority under any list of priorities that we may consider. Every important aspect of national life is inevitably and unfavorably affected by this malady.

Agriculture:

The nation must be fed. Only the monster of crime and corruption could conceivably be of equal or higher immediate priority than agriculture. This priority is very strongly supported by the **World Bank Report.** It is not at all surprising that an editorial in The Gleaner also substantiates the necessity to get people back into farming:

> *A call to action by the agricultural sector is being echoed across the reaches of Jamaica. First, there was a rallying cry for the expansion of honey production by no less a person than Minister of Agriculture Roger Clarke, who told of our inability to respond to the demand.*
>
> *And lately, food conglomerate GraceKennedy Limited urged increased production of peppers. And sector interests have also, from time to time, made a pitch for other produce such as ackee, cocoa and cassava.*

No one denies that agriculture is crucial to our progress as a self-sustaining nation. Over recent years Jamaica's agriculture has accounted for about 7% of GDP and just over 20% of employment. At the same time we import over US$800 million worth of foodstuff. There is economic as well as political sensitivity to this area of opportunity for import substitution. Very clearly, agriculture has great potential to become a much more significant contributor to employment and export earnings. The priority of the sector cannot be in doubt. In this case as well, there is a daunting question: Why have we not been able to feed ourselves and get those that abandoned farming to return to the land? **Vision 2030 Jamaica** acknowledges that although some improvement is noted in the Agriculture Production Index, the sector is off track and continues to fail to meet targets set. This dilemma is recognized and addressed in the excerpt below:

> *Given the potential contribution of agriculture to GDP, employment, the enhancement of rural livelihoods, environmental sustainability and food security, the sector occupies an important position in the planning for **Vision 2030 Jamaica**. Our long-term vision is for the dynamic transformation*

of the Jamaican agricultural sector through a sustained, research oriented, technological, market driven and private sector-led revolution, which revitalizes rural communities, creates strong linkages with other sectors and emphatically repositions the sector in the national economy to focus on production of high value commodities and contribute to national food security.

Tourism:

Because of the country's ongoing substantial commitment, the consistent annual growth rate of the sector as well as its individual contribution to foreign exchange earnings, tourism has to be seen as very high on the scale of priorities as well. An article in **The Jamaica Observer** of September 23, 2011 indicates Jamaica's earnings from tourism: *"Up to August Jamaica had earned US$1.480 billion which represents a 3.4 per cent increase over the US$1.432 billion we earned for the same period in 2010."* The direct contribution of tourism to GDP is about 10% and is expected to continue to grow at a rate of 2% to 4% per year.

Education:

While the direct, real-time contribution of education and training to the nation's wellbeing is never immediately or readily discernible there is no question that both are essential to the near and long-term viability of the nation. There is not a chance that Jamaica could ever join the ranks of the developed world without having an educated and well trained workforce. The **World Bank Report** indicates that the visible shortfall in what is called human capacity reflects our ongoing failure to educate and train our people. Thus education and training become crucial imperatives regardless of whether we attain the status of a developed country by 2030 or 2050, or not at all.

Conclusion:

For obviously practical reasons I do not believe that we can realistically expect to address any additional supportive goals as top priorities effectively at this time or in the very near future for that matter. This is not to say that we should abandon the other important goals. It simply means that we should defer them purposely on account of lack of resources and in order to improve our chances of success at our selected top priorities. It is much better to attend to three or four critical priorities diligently than to attempt to address ten or twelve reluctantly, always deeply apprehensive of the likelihood of success in all or even a majority of these.

However, if there were a single additional item that could be considered for inclusion in this group this would have to be the matter of our system of taxation. Historically, this has been a matter of the greatest concern but it has never been more pressing an issue than it is currently as Jamaica negotiates with the IMF in its attempts to find a way out of the fiscal quagmire in which it finds itself. Tax collection is a genuine rival for inclusion in the list of top priorities. Because of its clear importance I will attempt to address the issue in a manner that may yet treat it with the seriousness it deserves without creating a competitive relationship with the four core priorities identified. Commentary by a local financial analyst in **The Gleaner** of February 12, 2013 demonstrates, among other things, the significance of the collection of taxes:

> *Financial analyst Neilson Rose says the second debt exchange being introduced by the Government could give it the necessary space it needs for a year or two if the right things are done. Rose said it was critical that the Government move decisively to collect taxes due from everyone, fight against corruption, cut waivers and install the public-private sector oversight committee for the debt exchange.*

The **World Bank Report** comments at some length on Jamaica's very serious problems regarding taxation. The basic contention is that the tax system in Jamaica is as inefficient and inequitable as it is increasingly complex and cumbersome. Despite efforts at reforms, the conclusion is that:

> *Jamaica has one of the worst tax systems in the world, ranking 173rd out of 181 countries in the overall ease of paying taxes, 175th in the number of required annual tax payments, 148th in the time required to pay taxes,*

and 133rd in the total tax rate. For example, tax compliance for a typical company is estimated on average to take a total of 414 hours each year in Jamaica, compared to only 76 hours per year in Ireland and 61 hours in St. Lucia. During the medium term, fundamental tax reform will involve reducing the complexity of the system, reducing the time and number of payments required, and ensuring that horizontal and vertical equity is achieved.

On the subject, we will see that there is at least one compensatory approach that could win us time to address the issue of tax collection. This approach has to do with the crippling financial cost of corruption. It is estimated by some that corruption may account for as much as 90% of our national debt. Since corruption is to be addressed as one of our core priorities we may reasonably defer dealing with our tax collection problem at the very outset. Limiting the effect of corruption will allow us to improve our GDP significantly. In this way we mitigate the negative impact of low tax revenues and free up the resources that would be required to address this problem as a core priority. Integral to this deferral would be the sternest of warnings to all current and future transgressors that the penalties for evasion will be retroactively applied. In the interim we could make an offer of amnesty to those that voluntarily make amends before the next round of collection efforts is set in motion.

In the midst of all this we are haunted by the frightening reality that the extent to which we succeed in addressing crime and corruption will determine the extent to which we succeed at the other critical top priorities. Note the inclusion of corruption as a clearly acknowledged concern in the Gleaner commentary above. Interestingly, the identified top priorities provide us with the acronym CATE that offers great potential for powerful messaging in a slogan; for example: *Let's take care of CATE; CATE is the core; CATE is the cure.* This observation may be seen to be less than an important or integral part of our discussion but it really is not. It is perhaps impossible to overestimate the critical nature of the marketing of these priorities and their crucial value to our desired progress.

ii. Crime [Including Corruption]

Crime and corruption are Siamese twins. There is no doubt in my mind that any separation can only be a contrivance. Because of the hubris of privilege and the historical advantage of hierarchical authority, the powerful and corrupt have steadfastly refused to tolerate being termed or classified as common criminals and so the category of corruption is deferentially maintained. The truth is that in both intent and effect the practitioners of corruption are no different from the common criminal.

The contrived difference survives linguistically mainly on account of the influence of the powerful and the endless sycophancy of the beneficiaries of the corrupt. In the eyes of the man in the street, as ably exemplified in the NIA video introduced later in this discussion, the corrupt is unequivocally seen as no different from the common criminal. More and more the society at large is demanding that those guilty of corruption, convicted or not, be seen as undifferentiated criminals and be treated accordingly by the system of justice. Nonetheless, it is convenient to discuss the twins separately mainly because of the visible difference in where they originate and generally reside in our society.

Once again we witness a commonality between the Third World landscape and that of the First World as exemplified by the United States of America. In spite of the universal acknowledgement that Wall Street is the prime locus of the cause of the recent worst recession in American history, the agents of Wall Street have suffered little to no public retribution because of their place in hierarchy and the willingness of the power grid of which they are an integral part, to treat them with undue deference. Yet, a large enough segment of America now sees Wall Street and its agents as plain criminals even as we attempt to digest the recent admission by U.S. Attorney General, Eric Holder, that certain complicit, corrosive, large corporations and their officers are *too big* to prosecute. This, of course, is in keeping with the newly minted capitalist theory that these entities are *too big to fail*.

94

So grave, pervasive and destabilizing is the impact of crime that **Vision 2030 Jamaica** highlights this in addressing its number two goal of a Secure, Cohesive and Just Society. It is critical that we appreciate the magnitude of the excerpt below:

> *"**Vision 2030 Jamaica** will increase our sense of security by transforming our society into one which conforms to the rule of law, respects the rights of all, and coalesces around a set of shared values. Violent crimes have become one of the most pressing concerns for Jamaicans. It has had a negative impact on all spheres of society and has been cited as a significant factor in the low levels of GDP recorded by Jamaica over the years. It has left segments of our society crippled with fear and has resulted in the reallocation of budgetary resources into crime prevention and control. Private firms are forced to pay large sums of money for security, and in some instances, extortion fees. Community members are sometimes unable to pursue gainful occupations and schooling due to the impact of gang violence in their communities."*

It should be shocking to us that 50 years after Independence there is still need to transform our society into one that *conforms to the rule of law*. The fact that such a statement is necessary at this time substantiates the obviously endemic nature of crime in our society and unequivocally supports the inclusion of the subject among the top priorities that must be addressed with urgency. Vision **2030 Jamaica** also comments at length on the history of crime and the unyielding nature of its assault on the state and its citizens. The excerpt below comments on the alarmingly high murder rate and the impact of garrison communities:

High Murder Rate

> *While Jamaica's total crime rate declined over the last ten years, violent crimes have been increasing at a disconcerting rate. The murder rate, in particular, has almost doubled in every decade since Independence.*

In 2000, the country's murder rate was approximately 33 per 100,000 persons. By 2008, it had risen (despite fluctuations) to 60 per 100,000, among the three highest in the world. This fact has had a crippling effect on the society and has fuelled a strong sense of victimization and fear of crime in Jamaica. Although close to 90 per cent of the murders are committed on males, the number of females murdered has been increasing. In 2007, the number was 147; it rose to 164 in 2008. In contrast to the trends in murder, the general crime rate has been steadily declining. In 1996, the rate was 2,256 offences per 100,000.

By 2006, this rate had declined to 1,074. However, in 2007, the rate rose to 1,244 and preliminary indications are that it rose further in 2008. Nonetheless the earlier trend clearly focuses the concern on violent crimes and murder in particular. The society has puzzled over the factors that have led to the high murder rate. In some quarters, poverty and unemployment have been named as the main causes. However, while links have been established between the incidence of poverty and unemployment and certain types of crimes, there is little or no evidence to support the notion that the murder rate is the direct result of these factors. Two main factors that have been pinpointed are the ease of illegally accessing guns and the rise in criminal gang networks.

Dons and Garrison Communities

The advent of political "garrisons" and the attendant rise of the community "dons" have contributed to the proliferation of community gangs and murders. Garrison communities first arose in the 1960s as outcomes of a polarized political culture. This type of polarization resulted in the death of over 800 people during the 1980 General Elections. Many of these communities have evolved into havens for criminal gangs with the dons operating as leaders of criminal networks.

Not surprisingly, **Vision 2030 Jamaica** does not mention the universally acknowledged link between crime and politics. This omission does not minimize the importance of the commentary but it does leave one with a feeling of discomfort as to the willingness of the state to address the matter, especially when performance against crime reduction targets is declared to be *Off track, no improvement or worsening from baseline*. Though unlikely, it is possible that the plan's targets could be met. However, it will only be met at significant cost, with extraordinary political leadership and unusual national commitment.

An excerpt from the now very familiar **World Bank Report** further makes the point:

Crime is the most evident and severe problem in Jamaica

Once crime is established, it is difficult to overcome. It severely limits future growth and leads to a vicious circle as low growth further increases crime and higher crime rates further reduce growth. Crime erodes social stability and makes rule of law a critical area of concern. It has a negative effect on human capital, creating incentives for migration among the most skilled, educated, and entrepreneurial citizens. It constrains business expansion and diverts resources from productive activities to crime protection.

Because of crime and other structural conditions, investment in Jamaica tends to flow into isolated activities. All-inclusive resorts, mining, and Export Free Zones are the best examples of this enclave development model with its low spillovers (while tourists avoid crime-ridden areas, their dollars remain in the resort; mining communities and international businesses are similarly isolated from the greater Jamaica). A 2007 United Nations World Bank study illustrates the link between growth and lower crime rates. It states that Jamaica could experience an annual increase of 5.4 percent in per capita GDP, if it cut crime rates to the levels prevailing in Costa Rica.

An excerpt from the online news service, **Caribbean 360,** March 17, 2013, captioned, ***More must be done to arrest Caribbean drug trade says US,*** explains the complex and pervasive nature of our problem:

> *The US said that Jamaica remains the largest Caribbean supplier of mari-juana to the United States, adding that while cocaine and synthetic drugs are not produced locally, the country is a transit point for drugs trafficked from South America to North America and other international markets.*
>
> *It said that, in 2012, drug production and trafficking were both "enabled and accompanied by organized crime, domestic and international gang activity, and police and government corruption," adding that the gun trade for illicit drugs "exacerbated the problem as handguns moved into the country in exchange for drugs".*
>
> *Washington said marijuana from Jamaica is "increasingly being trafficked to Caribbean nations as well" and that "some Central American drug traf-ficking organizations exchange Jamaican marijuana for cocaine".*

Corruption:

In the Jamaican context, forensically speaking, crime is generally seen as nec-essarily physical, violent, and even brutal, in nature. It is also believed to leave in its path sufficient traces of evidence that may be pursued in steps toward the ulti-mate apprehension of the perpetrators, who are most often assumed to be from the lower classes of society.

Corruption is generally seen as quite different though quite often related. It is usually distinctly non-physical in nature, may engage physical violence from time to time as a means of ensuring its objectives are achieved, always involves significant sums of money and/or coercive influence, more often than not is connected to poli-tics, political figures and others in positions of authority and is usually seen as being in the domain of the upper classes. It is also the commonly held view that perpetrators, though seldom unknown, are rarely if ever prosecuted even when accused or charged. Most infuriating of all is the fact that even if pursued for protracted periods of time these villains are never brought before the local courts for trial.

In a remarkably well produced and documented hour long video, **The Cost of Corruption:** *Jamaica's Barrier to Prosperity*, the highly commendable local group **National Integrity Action** (NIA) lays bare the extraordinary, endemic nature of corruption and its blatant connection to politics. The authenticity of the video is reinforced by the diversity and status of the people that comprise its featured commentators. These include known and respected names such as: Professors Trevor Monroe and Anthony Clayton of the University of the West Indies (UWI), Arnold Bertram, former PNP minister of government, Senator Marlene Malahoo Forte, former judge and former JLP Minister of State for Foreign Affairs and Foreign Trade, Chris Zacca, president of the Private Sector Organization of Jamaica, Peter John Thwaites, chairman of Crime Stop, dub poet and radio personality Mutabaruka, and a number of unidentified man-in-the-street individuals. It is noteworthy that the video ends with messages of goodwill from the Governor General, the Prime Minister and the Leader of the Opposition. This panoply of contributors must surely prevent the tendency among many to wish to kill the messenger rather than pay attention to the message, especially when malfeasance is very clearly ascribable to either political party.

The video is easily accessible on line at *niajamaica.org*. It is a video every Jamaica stakeholder should view. Among the substantial examples of corruption provided by the video are **The DaCosta Commission Report 1973** ['*The Report of the Commission of Enquiry into the Award of Contracts, the Grant of Work Permits and Licences and Other Matters*'] and the findings on **Operation PRIDE,** a housing-for-the-poor program that turned out to be an unmitigated disaster. Both reveal corruption of such colossal proportions that even the passage of time cannot erase them from memory or minimize their lasting impact on the pernicious trend of the scourge of corruption that plagues our country. There can be no doubt that these examples more than amply demonstrate the claim that corruption is indeed Jamaica's barrier to prosperity.

Briefly, the DaCosta Commission primarily had to do with the awarding of contracts for the building of schools with a World Bank loan of around ten million dollars. The most dramatic corruption-facilitating subterfuge was the modification of the contract-granting protocol from oversight by a national panel to one that allowed individual Members of Parliament (MPs) to recommend contractors to build schools in their own constituencies. Inevitably, the duration and cost of the program doubled and only half the number of schools was built. Partisan political award of contracts and kickbacks to politicians were the common forms of abuse.

Twenty years after the school-building debacle, and for identical reasons, a project for low-income housing, **Operation PRIDE**, was launched under the aegis of the defunct National Housing Development Corporation. Plagued by allegations of corruption and mismanagement, the project saw the disappearance of about seven billion dollars. The then Minister of Housing, Dr. Karl Blythe, resigned in the wake of a damning report from a four-member investigating committee. The report suggested that Blythe acted improperly as minister with responsibility for the programme. Irregularities benefited fake contractors and fleeced those who were supposed to be beneficiaries. The commission reported that huge cost over-runs were incurred by *putting politics first with competence, need and merit second.*

Having learned nothing from this experience, in 2012 the government attempted to resurrect the project. It is no secret that since 2006, the Special Investigation Reports of the Office of the Contractor General have been *replete with evidence of corruption, at the level of the Parliament, the Parish Councils* and other public sector entities. One report states: *Yet only two successful prosecutions have emanated from more than 40 special investigation reports. In one case involving allegations of trans-national bribery of a former Member of Parliament pending since 2009, no decision has yet been announced as to prosecute or not to prosecute.* Importantly, the report points out that the impunity of the corrupt is reflected in the fact that 10 years prior to Independence three Ministers of Government were convicted of corruption, but 50 years since only a single one has been successfully prosecuted.

In a discussion paper, *Voice, Participation and Governance in a Changing Environment - The Case of Jamaica,* June 2000, by University of the West Indies

100

professor Trevor Munroe, sponsored by the **Caribbean Group for Cooperation in Economic Development** [CGCED], we learn the following:

> *A significant number of persons see corruption as a major threat to democracy in Jamaica. Over 48% of the persons interviewed in a survey conducted on behalf of The Gleaner Company by Don Anderson and his team from Market Research Services Ltd., indicate so. The survey was conducted over the period 18th to 21st April, 1999 and involved interviews amongst a nationally representative sample of 1000 persons aged 15 years and over in all parishes.*

Then there is the previously mentioned more recent case of Christopher Coke as well as that of David Smith of OLINT Corporation who swindled hundreds of Jamaicans through a Ponzi scheme while personally benefiting to the tune of some two hundred and twenty million U.S. dollars. Both these characters donated generously to both political parties. It therefore comes as no surprise that neither was ever brought to justice in Jamaica. Instead, they were extradited by American authorities, tried and sentenced to prison in the United States of America. The greatest of ironies is that more damage was done to Jamaicans in Jamaica than to any other group on account of the activities of these two criminals yet the U.S. had the first and maybe the only chance at prosecuting them. It is unlikely that any charges will ever be brought against them in Jamaica.

The outcome of the 2006 case of the Free Cuban Light Bulbs Project appears to give the lie to the contention that cases of corruption involving the political elite are seldom if ever pursued to their ultimate judicial conclusion. On closer examination, however, rather than assuaging our misgivings this case may actually justify them. Kern Spencer, the young junior minister, had responsibility for the light bulb project under Phillip Paulwell's Ministry of Industry, Technology, Energy and Commerce. He and others were accused of fraudulently selling four million light bulbs that were donated by the Cuban government to be distributed to consumers free of cost. The evidence indicates that the government ended up being liable for J$276 million or about US$4 million on account of the 'free' light bulbs. The charges in the case included three charges of conspiracy to defraud, one charge for breaching the Prevention of Corruption Act, and three charges for breaching the Money Laundering Act. Amazingly, in March of 2014 the trial judge dismissed the case on the basis that there was no case to answer.

It is very telling that the lead line of the **Jamaica Observer**, in its **Editorial** of March 27, 2014, reads: *The Kern Spencer verdict: '...the law is a ass -- a idiot!'* The editorial then goes on to say: *This quotation from Charles Dickens' 1838 novel, Oliver Twist, is hard to avoid when considering Monday's verdict in the Kern Spencer case.* Admirably, the paper urges caution as it attempts to avoid being accused of coming to a baseless conclusion in support of what the majority of observers also see as a travesty. Still, its commentary in this regard is highly instructive and is worthy of reproduction here:

We have no doubt that the long history of political corruption in Jamaica is driving the view that Mr. Kern Spencer is guilty of corruption in the Cuban light bulb fiasco.

But as tempting as it is to dismiss Mr. Spencer and his co-accused, Ms. Coleen Wright, as being guilty as charged, we must urge caution. We are a nation of laws and not of men.

For that very reason, we are strongly in favour of the prosecution being given the right of appeal, similar to the defence. This will allow a case to be tried to its final conclusion. Right now, as it is, "the law is a ass -- a idiot!"

We may see Spencer as uniquely unfortunate when it is considered that during the PNP's unbroken 18 years in government, according to the article, **Erasing The Corruption Stain**, in The Gleaner of Sunday, July 4, 2010, *there is no question that it served up a full menu of so-called scandals.* Spencer, how-ever, was the only official to be prosecuted on a range of criminal charges. Serious, widespread suspicions also surrounded the involvement of former Prime Minister P.J. Patterson and PNP officer Vin Lawrence in the Shell waiver and Sandals Whitehouse scandals, respectively. Other scandals involved Information Minister Colin Campbell in the Trafigura Affair and the earlier mentioned Technology Minister, Phillip Paulwell, in the NetServ controversy.

Regrettably, there are hundreds of examples of such abuse of office in Jamaican politics. Just as regrettably, only a paltry few are ever prosecuted and even fewer are pursued to their full judicial conclusion. Professor Anthony Clayton estimates that these types of corruption may account for perhaps as much as 90% of our accumulated national debt. Other frightening consequences with long-term implications include what the NIA so accurately describes as *the ruination of hundreds of Jamaican professionals and the tarnishing of the system of justice in Jamaica.*

All in all, the cost of crime and corruption to the nation is incalculable, intolerable and unsustainable. If we were limited to doing but a single thing toward the betterment of the nation, there can be no doubt that addressing crime and corruption effectively would have to be that single thing. There can be no doubt as to where our attack on the *status quo* must begin. Trinidad and Tobago, for example, appears to recognize the potential for its crime problem to escalate to the stage of Jamaica's and has recently passed laws to enable their army to exercise police powers under certain specified circumstances. This is clearly one approach to addressing the *status quo* in regard to the matter of law enforcement in the face of increasing crime rates.

iii. Responsibility: Dispersed but Orchestrated

Vision 2030 Jamaica is a project of such fundamental national significance that responsibility for its implementation and desired success cannot reside only among the leadership class. Such an allocation is all but guaranteed to invite failure at every important level. There is no substitute for the complete immersion of the general population in the critical details of the project and their subsequent commitment to its implementation and success. The level of difficulty associated with this requirement, though great, is impossible to measure with any certainty; more so because of our past halfhearted efforts at similar exercises, our evident reluctance to assess performance, communicate outcomes and hold responsible parties accountable.

The convergence of economic necessity, political vulnerability and diminishing optimism among a large number of citizens could be seen at this particular time as either a monumental challenge or an ideal opportunity to advance the dispersion of responsibility. I prefer to see the situation as offering challenging opportunity. This speculation is based partly on the fact that there is residual goodwill from the process by which the plan was developed. There was unusual bipartisan input and hence bipartisan support for the plan, there were contributions from a wide cross section of stakeholders and what appears to be muted expectation that the fundamentals of **Vision 2030 Jamaica** will be seen as a genuine, good- faith, last-ditch effort to address acknowledged intractable problems that were heretofore ignored or simply given lip service. Of course, it could simply be that we have suddenly come to realize that after digging a hole for ourselves over all these years it is time we cease digging. In any case, the man in the street must be convinced that the plan's objectives will be pursued with unusual conviction, diligence and honesty and that accountability for outcomes will be publicly acknowledged routinely on a timely basis.

Naturally, this does not in any way release the government specifically, or its agents and political leadership generally, from what in the final analysis is truly their particular crucial responsibility - ensuring that the plan is effectively implemented and the promised outcomes achieved. Closest to the government's level of responsibility is that of the non-government segment of the leadership class that, not unreasonably, should be expected to be a watchful partner whose non-political and likely independent interests should allow this group of stakeholders to participate vigorously in the valuable function of extra-governmental oversight.

The general responsibility of the public should then be to pay close attention to performance against objectives and complain vociferously when timelines are ignored or should failure appear imminent. There are some eight independent talk show radio stations over which a large number of disgruntled Jamaicans frequently and relentlessly voice their criticism of government and opposition alike. Here is a chance for this medium to channel the views of the people in a much more useful and focused way toward the goal of achieving the selected top priorities of **Vision 2030 Jamaica**.

Essentially, the quality of government leadership that is applied to the marketing and implementation of the plan will determine the degree to which it succeeds or fails. More to the point, however, is the realization that in the end the Prime Minister must bear the ultimate responsibility and be singularly accountable for all outcomes.

If we consider all stakeholders an orchestra, then the Prime Minister is the conductor. This is an inescapable responsibility given the nature of political organization. Regardless of which political party forms the government and who holds the position of Prime Minister, it must be understood and accepted by all that the buck stops with the incumbent Prime Minister.

iv. Nationalization vs. Politicization

There is the ever present danger in Jamaica that general disenchantment will ensue should a government orchestrated plan encounter difficulty or demand some sacrifice of the electorate. It is distinctly possible, in fact likely, that the people will withdraw their fickle support as well as seek to ascribe blame politically should things go awry. It is therefore imperative that **Vision 2030 Jamaica** be seen by the public at large and marketed by the government as totally bipartisan and entirely national in nature and scope. Parochial interests cannot be countenanced; neither can there be room or tolerance for even the insinuation that the plan is attributable to one party or the other. In other words, politicization must be absolutely taboo and avoided at all cost. The plan must always be indifferent and openly hostile to partisan desires or inclinations.

At the same time every instrument of acculturation must be utilized to inculcate the nation in the nonpartisan, nationalist nature of the plan and the absolute necessity that every citizen becomes vested in the plan as a guardian of its marketing, implementation and success. These instruments should include every primary, secondary and tertiary educational institution, every social/business club such as the Boys' Scouts, Girls' Guides, Jaycees, Rotary, Kiwanis, Lions, Optimist, Chamber of Commerce and certainly all clubs identified as Ladies' Clubs. Universal evidence indicates that women are much better at endeavors such as this. Jamaican women undoubtedly confirm this fact. A summary of the plan should be on the walls of every school room and associated buildings, and flyers should be widely distributed throughout the country from time to time. The plan and its priorities should be displayed tastefully in every appropriate public space. The plan should be integrated into the appropriate sections of every school curriculum and be a part of related examination schedules. In short, the plan must be treated as a tool of war against what should be seen as a destructive, national-health epidemic - addiction to the *status quo* and all of its debilitating side effects. The truth may well be that we are in fact engaged in the war of our lives - the war for our very survival as a viable, exemplary nation.

The very low level of active awareness of **Vision 2030 Jamaica** currently, is very surprising and of great concern as indeed it should be to its framers and the government that must surely be seen as its singular sponsor. Not many Jamaicans with whom I speak at home or abroad seem to be aware of the plan let alone its scope and profound significance to the island's future. Some more cynical souls readily explain that plans such as **Vision 2030 Jamaica** are routinely prepared solely for effect, with no commitment to execution or expectation that they will ever be implemented. In other words, these are political ploys or plans of convenience meant to satisfy the influential external overseers of our fiscal performance such as the World Bank and IMF. Regrettably, history does support this claim. Still, we do need to get to a place in our national psyche that requires that we place a stop loss on our investment in hope. We must not lose faith in hope especially when, now more than ever, it does appear that hope is ironically the most substantial and perhaps the only currency in our national survival arsenal that is yet to be devalued and remains uniquely under our direct, unassailable control. Hope is what may yet lead us out of the doldrums of our ever-increasing despair. **Vision 2030 Jamaica** does provide some basis for hope.

v. Counting The Cost

While the cost of implementing **Vision 2030 Jamaica** has not been determined with any specificity, it is reasonable to assume that whatever this may turn out to be, the cost of not implementing the plan would be at least equivalent. However, given the gross negative implications of failure to implement the plan, it is more than likely to be the case that this cost will exceed the probable cost of implementation. The top priorities of Crime, Agriculture, Tourism and Education identified earlier are of such great value to the nation's well-being that failure to act on these fronts at this time or at the very earliest opportunity is likely to do irreparable harm to the country's desired progress.

In fact, as mentioned earlier, the opportunity cost of our previous failures to implement similar national plans is really cumulative. This, therefore, makes failure at implementing the current and most ambitious of plans painfully additive. This is an expensive proposition and one that should stimulate and encourage much greater effort and commitment on this occasion. At the same time we cannot ignore the implications of our current state of affairs, especially as this is bound to be unfavorably affected by whatever agreement is arrived at with the IMF. It is probable that **Vision 2030 Jamaica** will be shelved in order that we tend to the current fiscal crisis that forced us into negotiations with the IMF in the first place. There is no denying the validity and urgency of this priority given historical as well as current international financial arrangements. As well, there is no denying the fact of our resource poverty and the overwhelming evidence that as a country we continue to be extremely poorly managed. Still, what we must not do is to abandon the project altogether. This would be the most terrible of mistakes and one of historic proportions. In fact, **Vision 2030 Jamaica** should become one of the main drivers of the desire to get our national house in order this time.

6

THE DIASPORA

There are as many Jamaicans in the Diaspora as there are Jamaicans at home. The United States, the United Kingdom and Canada are the major Diaspora centers. If for no other reason but sheer numbers, these Jamaicans have significant political as well as economic influence both in their host countries and in Jamaica. The impact of the group on Jamaica's economy literally makes the Jamaican Diaspora Jamaica's quiet knight in shining armor. The *March 2010 Bank of Jamaica Remittance Update* from the **External Sector Statistics Unit**, indicates that in spite of the economic battering inflicted by the worldwide recession on Jamaicans abroad, especially in the United States, remittances by the Diaspora declined, 2009 over 2008, by a relatively modest 7%. However, for 2010 over 2009 this was reversed dramatically by an increase of 6.5%, according to a commentary in **The Gleaner** of June 12, 2011: *Jamaican Diaspora a key partner for economic growth.* Total formal remittances represent the largest single source of foreign-exchange inflows amounting to about 13% of total GDP. Remittances as reported by the World Bank totaled about US$2 billion in 2007. This more than doubled the US$892 million in 2000 and demonstrates a level of commitment and patriotism that is nothing short of remarkable. Particularly, it demonstrates a love of family and respect for those at home whose sacrifices made the members of the Diaspora succeed to the extent that they have succeeded and continue to succeed.

In a May 22, 2013 **Jamaica National Bank** news release, the measure of the immense significance of the Diaspora is abundantly clear:

> Jamaicans in the Diaspora are of strategic importance to Jamaica in its quest for sustainable development; and the major indicators of its value in this process are: remittances which represent 17% of GDP, and tourists which is some 11-15% of overall visitors. That, according to the Jamaica Diaspora Institute (JDI), the operating arm of the Jamaica Development Foundation (JADF), in its assessment leading up to the 5th Biennial Jamaica Diaspora Conference, to be held in Montego Bay, June 16-19, 2013.

> Professor Neville Ying, Executive Director of the JDI, said that there are numerous Diaspora organizations, which make significant contributions to Jamaica in healthcare, education, sports, business, investment and trade. And, there are some 132 recorded health missions from the Diaspora, which provide free health care services especially in rural communities, and the donation of equipment and pharmaceutical supplies to hospitals and health clinics. "We estimate that approximately 131 alumni associations in the Diaspora contribute scholarships, donate equipment and educational supplies; as well as, financial assistance for student welfare and infrastructure development projects to a variety of educational institutions in Jamaica," Professor Ying stated. And, he affirmed that the Jamaican government recognizes the importance of the Diaspora to the development of Jamaica.

Media all around the globe in countries in which Jamaicans are represented relate amazing stories of successful, prosperous Jamaicans. One such story by Royson James appears in the **Toronto Star** of November 03, 2012 in the **News / Insight** section. The title of the story, *Most Torontonians of Jamaican descent a* *boon to the city,* exemplifies the prevalence and diversity of Diaspora success and prosperity. Notably, the first paragraph of the story gives the lie to the somewhat overexposed falsehood that the majority of Jamaicans abroad are less than honorable as residents and citizens. To the contrary, James says: *Beyond the gangsters and punks are thousands of successful Torontonians of Jamaican descent, physicians, lawyers, tycoons, judges, professors, plumbers, teachers, TTC* [Toronto Transit Commission] *operators.* To emphasize the point, James goes on to mention billionaire Michael Lee-Chin among 50 well-known stars in the Diaspora firmament but marvels at the fact that there is a very long list of others that failed to make the list of 50 but just as easily could. Among these are people like Alvin Curling, former Minister of Housing, Province of Ontario, Professor Carl James and writer Rachel Manley. Using a baseball analogy, James concludes justifiably that *The bench is deep* in regard to examples of tremendous success among the Diaspora.

Yet another demonstrative example of the impact of the Diaspora is visible in *One People - The Celebration Documentary,* produced by Justine Henzell and Zachary Harding in celebration of Jamaica's 50th Independence Anniversary in 2012. The documentary showcases successful and prosperous Jamaicans on every continent and in places as diverse as Kenya, China, Saudi Arabia and Russia. Jamaicans are literally making their mark everywhere! The one universally discernible fact is that they are all relentlessly and unapologetically proud to be Jamaican. It is obligatory that in any approach to addressing Jamaica's problems and opportunities we consider the actual and potential influence, role and impact of this remarkable group.

In spite of this extraordinary view of the Diaspora, an excerpt from an article by Daraine Luton in The Gleaner of June 17, 2013, on the occasion of the fifth biennial Jamaica Diaspora Conference in Jamaica, exemplifies the complexity, discomfort and confusion in the relationship between local political forces and the Diaspora. Opposition spokesman on foreign affairs and foreign trade, Dr. Christopher Tufton, is quoted by Luton as saying: *For some Diaspora persons, it* [the Conference] *represents a nice holiday; for some, it represents a nice social event to have a drink and visit family."* Tufton is also quoted as saying: *While all of that is important, the fundamental role and feature of the Diaspora approach that we should be pursuing now is to find out* **how we can use** *the Diaspora to achieve growth and development.* I have highlighted a section of the last quote that reveals a not too uncommon notion of how the Diaspora's purpose is perceived. At best the phrase is unfriendly; at worst it is Machiavellian. Neither is helpful in improving the relationship and leveraging the opportunities the Diaspora obviously presents.

a.   Collaboration or Mobilization?

There is a registered entity known as the **Jamaican Diaspora** that meets biennially in Jamaica under the auspices of the Government of Jamaica. The entity operates under the management of an Advisory Board. The Board comprises representatives from the centers of major Diaspora populations. As should be expected, the Government of Jamaica, through its Ministry of Foreign Affairs & Foreign Trade, is a direct and committed supporter of **Jamaican Diaspora**. There also exists at the University of the West Indies (UWI) a **Jamaica Diaspora Institute** (JDI) whose operational arm is the **Jamaica Diaspora Foundation** (JADF). Interestingly, the Institute is a part of the UWI Mona School of Business. Among the major priorities of the JADF are the issues of dual citizenship and voting rights in Jamaica for members of the Diaspora, especially as this relates to the consideration of a *Diaspora senator*. As indeed it should be, the Jamaican Diaspora is recognized as being of extraordinary significance by all levels of Jamaican society.

Understandably, this acknowledged and obvious importance does bring some complexity and challenge to the relationship between the Diaspora and the government and its agencies. Indeed, politics is about nothing if not about the art of subtle and not so subtle control of any influential part of the body politic. In order to understand and appreciate the concern of the Jamaica Government in respect of the relationship, regardless of the party in power, a number of characteristics needs to be recognized and accounted for. These include differences in conditions in Diaspora host countries, the diversity of the group in terms of economic status, qualifications and age, native political party sympathies or

112

affiliation and points of interest in terms of critical economic and social issues at home in Jamaica.

The differences in Diaspora population size in a particular host country as well as proximity to Jamaica are also relevant as these affect the extent and immediacy of communications and travel and the transfer of gifts in kind such as clothing, light durable goods and airline tickets, for example. I suspect that these gifts are not generally reflected in dollar remittance numbers although they do impact the standard of living of large numbers of Jamaicans at home. This invisible aspect of remittances contributes directly as well to the dramatic expansion of street vendoring and informal trading in Jamaica. It also helps explain how noticeable numbers among the unemployed appear to *live well* in spite of their circumstances locally. It is generally true, nevertheless, that conditions in Diaspora host countries may not vary significantly enough one to another in any other respects to warrant extensive discussion here.

The economic status of the Diaspora is of particular interest because it allows a very significant degree of independence of thought and action on matters of national significance beyond the purely economic. It is unimaginable that the more enlightened Diaspora does not influence local thinking on such issues as corruption, gay rights and republic status, for example. In my experience, among the Diaspora, even large organized groups like social clubs or churches tend not to pay too much attention to political preferences in reacting to specific needs at home. This level of independence may be explained by the fact that there is no political dependency on the part of these individuals or groups among the Diaspora. In other words, their economic circumstances insulate them from the tribal nature of politics in Jamaica, including the coercive force of the selective distribution of scarce goods and services by political agents.

Together, the academic/professional qualifications and the age of the Diaspora and migrating population represent welcome opportunity as well as immense challenge for Jamaica. The opportunity lies in the dampening effect on population growth along with the massive economic benefits that accrue. The challenge lies in the unquestionably significant contribution to the brain drain. According to the paper **Country Profiles -** *Jamaica: From Diverse Beginning to Diaspora in the Developed World* by **Alex Glennie and Laura Chappell, Institute for Public Policy Research** for the **Migration Policy Institute's** (MPI) **Migration nation-transforming Source** (MIS), around 7 percent of all Jamaicans have university degrees, compared with 20 percent of males and 9 percent of females who migrate. In other words, the highly educated are disproportionately likely to migrate. Of importance as well is the dramatic change in the gender composition of those who join the Diaspora. The MPI terms this the *feminization of Jamaican migration.* Clearly, the improved levels of female education along with the changing labor markets overseas increasingly facilitate accelerated female migration. This trend is confirmed by Elizabeth Thomas-Hope in her paper, *Migration Situation Analysis, Policy and Programme Needs for Jamaica.* The paper indicates that from the 1970s through the early part of the first decade of this century, female migration has consistently accounted for more than 50% of migration. Coincidentally, the local Jamaica labor pool, especially at the highest executive levels, also mirrors this distinct feminization trend. Naturally, this is very disruptive of the traditional place and role of the Jamaican male in local culture. Both the cause and implications of this baffling change will be explored later.

The gender switch in migration pattern is readily discernible. Much less so is the age profile of the majority of immigrants and hence the make-up of the Diaspora. Thomas-Hope indicates that the three groups of ages 10-19, 20-29, 30-39, comprise 60% to more than 70% of immigrants to the major immigration centers over the three plus decades beginning in 1970. For a newly independent country such as Jamaica in particular, this phenomenon is cause for genuine concern because of its projected potential implications.

To the extent that local government and its agencies, institutions like the UWI and highly regarded private sector organizations such as GraceKennedy and Jamaica National Building Society remain engaged with the Diaspora in established, formal ways, there is meaningful and beneficial collaboration. However, it is my view that such collaboration is a halfway house in a relationship that must become visibly more robust, coordinated and focused. Collaboration will get to the low hanging fruit via short-term, relatively inexpensive projects, awards and blandishment. It will not get us to the necessary stage of mobilization of the entire Diaspora in support of a concerted, long-term assault on the major roadblocks in our way and the energetic, unyielding commitment to the major themes of our plan for survival. Think Israel. **Vision 2030 Jamaica** undoubtedly provides a very hopeful starting point in any attempt to mobilize the Diaspora for the long haul.

The ongoing discussions about Diaspora Bonds are very unlikely to bear fruit. No Jamaica government has ever done enough to cultivate and secure the level of faith and confidence necessary to attract this type of investment among the Diaspora to a degree that even comes close to expectations. Needless to say, the recent and current financial trials involving debt default on the very instruments in question are direct disincentives. It appears that a better proposition would be direct investment in private enterprise ventures in areas like education, agriculture and tourism. All of these are integral parts of **Vision 2030 Jamaica**.

b. Contribution and Influence

Diaspora contributions have been overwhelmingly on a person-to-person basis in support of expenses directly related to survival issues such as family emergencies, food, school fees and rent, for example. On this basis the influence of the Diaspora is as dispersed and unfocused as the current contributions regime. This inevitably disperses its influence rather than focuses it. In so doing the influence, while acknowledged as significant, is nevertheless minimized in terms of visible national impact. Once mobilization occurs, everything changes. It is always true that he who pays the piper puts himself in the best of positions to call the tune. This will present the local government with the greatest challenge of all because the relationship will now demand transparency and accountability. In this regard, the Diaspora is perhaps in the best position to mount a bold, frontal attack against the numbing *status quo*.

The challenge to government is evident in an article in The Gleaner of July 24, 2012 titled, *Let Diaspora Vote...But Jamaicans Reject Idea of Overseas*

Residents Sitting in Parliament. Clearly, the debate is already in progress and is unlikely to end anytime soon. I am unequivocally in support of allowing members of the Diaspora to vote in national elections. Commonwealth countries such as Australia and New Zealand already allow this. I am not in favor of allowing the Diaspora parliamentary representation but not for the reason most may assume. My lack of support for the idea is driven by a very profound concern that any such representative would likely be overwhelmed, coopted and corrupted by supporters of the *status quo* to such an extent that he would prove useless or even harmful to the cause. At this juncture I strongly opt for addressing Diaspora issues from arm's length via the ballot and through mobilization around the survival issues mentioned earlier.

It is not difficult to imagine an offshore **Diaspora Investment Clearing House** for social and other more traditional capital investments in Jamaica. With a highly selective and focused approach, the influence of the Diaspora would be immense under such a scheme. Such an innovation would also minimize political intrigue, and, to a significant extent, make more secure the integrity of Diaspora representatives. This arrangement would doubtlessly, almost inevitably, keep government performance and accountability in the spotlight of local as well as Diaspora public opinion.

While mobilized Diaspora contribution may not fully guarantee the degree of influence many may desire, it surely is the most likely to facilitate and foster the growth of such influence. When we get to the section where we propose a new way to govern, it will become much more apparent how critical and impactful the mobilized public opinion of the Diaspora may be.

c. Milch Cow or Savior?

Many among the Diaspora do contend that successive governments see the Diaspora as simply a rather large piggy bank that may be freely accessed from time to time as various needs arise or as various administrations determine. The Diaspora Bond issue does not escape being seen in this manner. Among the major reasons for this, of course, are the historical profligacy of successive administrations, the not uncommon default on bond payments as happened recently and the ongoing apparent unwillingness or inability of successive administrations to address some significant concerns of the Diaspora effectively over extended periods of time. Even governments must eventually recognize the reality that milch cows cease producing milk after a while, especially if abused or ignored.

Even as a milch cow, however, the Diaspora may also be seen as a savior and with some justification. In fact, it is not unreasonable to see the Diaspora as the donor of endless resort; the quintessential savior. The religious connotation is not without some significance. Like the Savior of religion, the Diaspora is always forgiving but for much more practical reasons. Although Diaspora remittances are as substantial as they are and mean so much to Jamaica's economy, these remittances are not controllable by any government or its agents since they go directly to individual beneficiaries. Until and unless the government convinces the Diaspora that it can be a much more reliable, performing and accountable instrument, the Diaspora will be very reluctant to funnel its remittances or even meaningful portions of these remittances through the government or any of its designated agencies.

It is very doubtful that the government will or can mend its ways on its own. The Diaspora will necessarily have to perform the function of reform instigator, the gadfly if you will, along with coopted resident beneficiaries who, understandably, will be instinctively opposed to having significant portions of their remittances transferred to or through the government. No one can reasonably assume that all remittances will ever be voluntarily transferred in this manner. One member of the government recently made this possibility so much more unattractive and remote by suggesting that a tax be applied to all remittances. This kind of thinking is so self-defeating that it borders on the absurd.

In the end we may conclude that the Diaspora is both milch cow and savior. The definitive challenge for government is to eradicate the milch cow image and minimize the likelihood that the Diaspora may be seen as a savior of first as well as last resort. More to the point, the government is obliged to minimize, if not eliminate altogether, the need for any kind of urgently necessary or clearly identifiable economic savior. This consideration leads us to the awareness that it is highly unlikely that the later descendants of the Diaspora will remain as connected and committed to Diaspora causes as their parents or grandparents.

This waning of generational connection and commitment is a natural and inevitable turn of events that should give pause and must be taken into account by both the current Diaspora and the government. This means that critical projects and long-term causes that currently have or may deserve Diaspora support in the future, must advance from isolated, project-style status and be integrated into institutionalized approaches and processes that provide real opportunity for trans-generational connection and commitment. This option further advances the cause of the need for a **Diaspora Investment Clearing House** as mentioned earlier.

The critical nature of linkages, whether generational or institutional, may be overlooked or misunderstood only at great peril and certainly more to the disadvantage of the homeland than of the Diaspora. It becomes crucial, therefore, that governments not only acknowledge this but immediately and vigorously pursue and engage the Diaspora on this account.

7

A PROFILING & EVENT CULTURE

Jamaican culture, especially in the area of entertainment, has always been firmly grounded in the people's African heritage. However, the roots of this heritage have been intentionally stripped, tapped and spliced, some may say abused, by the latest crop of entertainers. The result is a troubling hybridization with American popular entertainment culture in a superficially complex, almost revolutionary rejection of traditional mores along with a raw, raucous rebellion against the usual modes of dress, speech and comportment. The incentive seems to be the potential for securing increasingly profitable space in the rich American entertainment market and American popular culture in general.

Perhaps the most constant feature of this hybridization is an aggressive, erratic *nouvelle culture* that may best be described by a contemporaneous word: *bling*. Wikipedia defines the word as a *slang term popularized in hip-hop culture, referring to flashy, ostentatious or elaborate jewelry and ornamented accessories that are carried, worn or installed, such as cell phones or tooth caps*. The word aptly describes both the entertainment culture and its spillover effects in local culture generally. This is not an unusually speedy cause-and-effect relationship in Jamaica and nearly all Third World countries; thanks to the limitless effects of the Internet and social media. The impact is visible in the way many younger people dress, crass consumerism and a level of conspicuous consumption that directly contradicts obvious, pervasive poverty. For example, people who can hardly afford a single cell phone will be seen carrying two and many are known to choose purchasing a phone card over paying for a meal. Nowhere are the complexity, confusion and anthropological resonance of this new culture better observed and explained than in the scholarly work by Norman C. Stolzoff, **Wake the Town & Tell the People**: *Dancehall Culture in Jamaica.* Dancehall music, considered the predecessor of hip-hop, is the caldron for this *nouvelle culture.*

Given the constantly turbulent nature of this culture I see it as essentially transitory. None of its aspects appears to have great potential for permanence although the durability of the social and historical forces that seem to drive its always morphing character is undeniable. Dancehall culture is offensive to very many Jamaicans, particularly those of earlier generations. Its influence on the non-entertainment areas of the culture is nevertheless significant and disruptive. It is debatable whether this constant culture mutation is the cause or the result of our apparent national reluctance or inability to discern and understand potential criti-cal linkages in our society. What is indisputable is that these disconnects exist. It appears that we do not generally recognize the negative effects of the *nouvelle culture* on the behavior of the younger generation specifically; neither, for example, do we see the potential for positive outcomes in purposely establishing explicit linkages among traditionally unconnected enterprises like scholastic disciplines, athletic prowess, tourism, marketing, management and the entertainment industry.

This deficiency in insight makes us vulnerable to a tendency toward profiling behavior and a silo mentality that sees even considerable achievements as totally unrelated events rather than as a series of connected opportunities. For example, it should not be too much of a challenge to integrate the remarkable success of Jamaica's athletes into a national objective of interconnected excellence in areas like best practices, personal and team discipline in the workplace and the nation, assessment of performance against standards, the value of preparation in achieving set goals or targets and the power of modeling positive behavior.

It is admirable that the University of Technology (UTEC) actually has a Department of Sports. However, an examination of its program reveals that it is distinctly confined to sports. It is disappointing that it does not attempt to make the types of advantageous linkages alluded to when these clearly offer great potential to expand the scope of the program and allow meaningful growth opportunities beyond sports itself. This unnecessary limitation leads us to a concern that may or may not be directly related to our disconnected, unbalanced approach to sports and entertainment. Both are seen by far too many, especially young men, as the primary escape route from poverty. Yet, as we know, this is very unlikely to be the case, except for a very extraordinary few among these dreamers. We must parlay our world class prowess at sports and entertainment into an effective opportunity multiplier. This consideration cannot be usefully addressed without recognizing a most troubling change in Jamaican culture: the obvious, sharp decline in the status of men and the rapid advance in the status of women. Let me hasten to clarify that this is purely an observation and not a veiled expression of either preference or regret.

a.   The Status of Men vs. the Status of Women

In respect of the family, Jamaica has always been a matriarchal society. The environment in which I grew up in Jamaica as well as my own personal familial experience supports the observation. It is confirmed indisputably by Edith Clarke in the seminal work, **My Mother Who Fathered Me**. In regard to the broader society however, few would deny that the society was patriarchal. The use of the past tense is intentional since this is, in fact, no longer the case. The new reality is mirrored in nearly all fields of endeavor and most certainly in the halls of academia, the incubator of our future. In fact, in an article by Sarah Morrison, *Revealed: The best and worst places to be a woman,* in the March 4, 2012, edition of **The Independent**, a British newspaper, the role change is applauded:

> *Best place for high-skilled jobs: Jamaica*
> *Jamaica has the highest ratio of women in high-skilled jobs, such as legislators, senior officials and managers. Almost 60 per cent of these roles are filled by women.*

Not surprisingly, not everyone agrees with this claim. Dr. Marcia Forbes, a media specialist and co-owner of a multimedia production company in Jamaica, contradicts this view in a March 12, 2012 article, **Women in Jamaica**, in the **Caribbean Journal**. Forbes claims that the overwhelmingly large number of positions held by women is not in the area of high-skilled jobs. She asserts that just the opposite is the case. While the statistics do seem to support Forbes' contention currently, it does appear that the potential for women to overtake men in the area of high-skilled jobs is unquestionably very high, thus advancing the inevitability of the occurrence. Even Forbes accepts that at least 70% of university graduates are women and that *women occupy many middle and top-level jobs*. There can be no doubt that both conditions place women in a significantly more favorable position than men in terms of future progress.

In 2009 on a visit to Jamaica I stayed with friends in an upper middle class neighborhood in Red Hills, a mountain suburb of Kingston. After several morning walks I observed that women outnumbered men significantly in the number of them on the way to work and driving very expensive cars. I confirmed this disparity by doing a simple but indicative check for a few mornings. My sampling revealed that, on average, for every 20 expensive cars 17 were being driven by women. This was quite a surprise since as recently as 30 years earlier the reverse was certainly the case. Although this sampling cannot be seen as scientific, it is nevertheless clearly relevant and directionally instructive, especially when viewed against the favorable positioning of women in the workplace and in academia. There is no doubt in my mind that this trend contributes to the observable decline in the high-profile visibility and the formerly automatic transactional superiority of men. The speed at which this gender transition is occurring is obviously disruptive to traditional culture norms and, in my view, directly contributory to a dramatic increase in the level of male disrespect for and abuse of females as well as the alarming growth in crime generally. The sharp decline in the status of men is as undeniably clear as is the rapid advance in the status of women.

The plight of men, especially the youth in this demographic, is made painfully clear in the October, 2012 column by Henley Morgan, *Our men are killing us*, in the

Jamaica Observer. The following excerpt from the column is well worth our full attention and is surely cause for serious concern:

Jamaican youth, more specifically males, are in crisis.

The concern that our males, primarily in the 18 - 24 age group, are in crisis is neither misplaced nor exaggerated. Let's examine the extent of the crisis with the help of statistics from the Statistical Institute of Jamaica. In 2010 the population in Jamaica by gender was males, 1,332,700 (49.3 per cent) and females, 1,373,100 (50.7 per cent), almost even. Yet, females did better than males measured by almost every key indicator. Life expectancy at birth: males 68.57 years, females 75.3 years. Literacy rates for people 15 years old and over: total population 85.9 per cent, males 80.6 per cent and females 90.8 per cent. Student enrolment: Primary, males 51.1 per cent, females 48.9 per cent; Secondary, males 49.9 per cent, females 50.1 per cent; Tertiary, males 31.4 per cent, females 68.6 per cent. Victims of homicide: males 90 per cent, females 10 per cent. Perpetrators of homicide (people arrested): males 98.0 per cent, females 2.0 per cent.

As mentioned earlier, one of the most reliably authentic reflections of transformation in our traditional culture can be seen in the music and stories of the ordinary people. In this case, the lyrics of the now popular Dancehall music culture confirm the observation. Much of the music is misogynistic, homophobic and glorifies reckless sex and violent behavior. The conundrum is whether the lyrics simply reflect or actively stimulate prevailing behavior or conditions. This is a matter of constant controversy among many Jamaicans and doubtlessly marks a point of departure for those who consider themselves sophisticates and those they consider *butoos* or the hoi polloi, i.e. those severely lacking in the commonly accepted social graces. One confusing aspect of the new culture is that *butoos* and sophisticates may drive similarly expensive cars, wear similar designer clothes and live in the same neighborhoods. No longer does shade of skin, education or sophistication allow accurate class differentiation. In fact, it appears that among the most intentionally provocative attributes of the new culture is its purposeful disruption of the traditional social order. This provides a clear example of the effectiveness of intentional opposition to the *status quo* in achieving social change.

In this environment many men appear reluctant, unwilling or unable to compete with women for scarce, higher paying jobs. There is no doubt that there are now more qualified women available over a much wider range of professional opportunities than in the recent past. Compounding the problem for men is the fact that the job market is no longer partial to men. Patriarchy has lost its place, power and advantage as women have become increasingly more qualified and visibly more competitive and competent.

There is a curious paradox that results from the disappearance of male gender advantage. On the one hand, the population is generally in favor of this new gender equality. On the other, the expectation remains intact that men will continue to reap the fruits of an advantage they no longer enjoy. We should not lose sight of the immense dislocation, discomfort and social pressures that this situation naturally imposes on men. There are stories, for example, of resentful men asking their wives whom they had to sleep with in order to rise so rapidly up the corporate ladder. It is a fairly commonly held view that the unusual challenges presented by the unavoidable adjustments to the traditional image of the male contribute directly to the increasingly misogynistic behavior of men as well as to the growing sophistication and brutality of crime. It almost seems as if there is a refocusing of male brain power from lawful, legitimate pursuits to get-rich-quick schemes and shady endeavors even if violent crime has to be an instrument.

It is perhaps no coincidence that the U.S. authorities are investigating a huge Jamaican-based scamming cartel-like operation. America's **Fox News** indicates that according to the U.S. Federal Trade Commission the number of complaints from American citizens about Jamaican lottery fraud soared from 1,867 in 2007 to about 30,000 in 2012. Even the most conservative estimates put the yearly take from Jamaican scams at $300 million, up from about $30 million in 2009. A

U.S. Federal Trade Commission official believes the scams could now be bilking Americans out of up to $1 billion a year.

This type of crime is becoming much more prevalent and acceptable in Jamaica. Some Jamaicans are totally unsympathetic to the American victims and even see the ill-gotten gains as some sort of reparation for slavery. The entire scamming enterprise is symptomatic of the wider problem of national malaise and the inability of successive governments to manage the country's affairs in a manner that ensures personal as well as national viability and discourages nationally destructive deviant behavior by its citizens. It is instructive that the Jamaica Minister of National Security, Peter Bunting, visited the United States in his official capacity, in an attempt to mitigate the potential negative impact of the Jamaica scamming enterprise on the critical tourist industry.

b. Missing Links

Reference was made earlier to our inability to make connections among catalytic achievements like the world class performance of Jamaica's athletes or the international impact of Jamaican music. The associated dramatic irony so easily observed is that while the formal institutional structures that support education, industry and commerce, for example, do not make these linkages, the average youth automatically does so. Not only do the youth voice their desire to be athletes, singers or musicians but on their own they actually take steps to demonstrate the desire. All over the island children and young adults may be observed engaging in athletic activity such as running, jumping, boxing and soccer with the barest minimum of equipment and even less institutional assistance or support.

Because of the high visibility and national affection for these sports as well as the visible accompanying financial success and high regard associated with the ultra-successful practitioners of these sports, young people now place alarmingly high and destabilizing value on these activities. They see them as distinctly promising ways to escape their otherwise gloomy circumstances. In a word, they are self-motivated. This motivation should be harnessed by government and allied institutions in the society and channeled into purposely linked and nationally important activity such as education and training, for example. This is especially the case when we know that no more than a relatively small number of these singularly motivated youth can possibly achieve meaningful success in the field of entertainment, athletics or sports in general.

The continued isolation of catalytic activities and achievements will not only stymie individual as well as national progress but may refocus the positive desires of once motivated youth onto areas of unfavorable and generally negative activities such as those associated with crime.

c. The Marketing Enterprise

We need to change the way the world sees our country and its people. Obviously, this means that we need to market ourselves differently. Jamaica is not simultaneously and separately a tourist mecca, a music and entertainment powerhouse, the cradle of world class athletes, the home of the internationally significant Jamaica Diaspora, a best-in-class producer of marijuana and one of the most crime-riddled countries on the planet. Instead, what we are is whatever the inevitable blend of all these things reveals us to be. Unfortunately, as with all blends the character of the end product will always reflect the strength and proportion of the most potent ingredients. Regrettably, the Jamaica blend is characterized by the unpleasant scent of crime and corruption. James Bond, the character of films, is famous for asking that his drink be shaken not stirred; Jamaica's image needs to be shaken, stirred and strained. This may only be done when we come to understand that a nation thrives because of the combination of the wholeness and wholesomeness of its character.

In the old world, the world before the Internet and Facebook, we may have been able to market what we are not and yet get away with the charade. To some extent we have been lucky on this account. In the new world, however, this is generally impossible. While as a country we must become a focused marketing

126

enterprise, we are first obliged to recreate ourselves to ensure that we do have something of value to market. This is never easy, simple or fast. Similarly, what I will suggest as the most viable approach to our transformation will not be easy, simple or fast and will demand sacrifice and the willingness to embrace and pursue an unusual path.

Given the nature of the transformation we will be obliged to endure, it will be decidedly advantageous to simultaneously market both the envisioned transformation and the unusual methodology that will guide its implementation. In the meantime we must immediately begin to plan our marketing strategy by engaging all stakeholders in this monumental, transformative endeavor. We must begin to see our country as **Jamaica Marketing Enterprise Inc**.

d. Understanding The Competition

We are our greatest competition!

Consider this: In the most fundamental sense, our major competition is with ourselves – the self we must abandon and the self we must become. Needless to say, this is not a simple matter of separating our past from our future. The complexity arises because what must be abandoned is not totally differentiated as to good and bad or black and white. There are gradations. It will require immense skill in leadership and management to differentiate, select and retain the portions of our culture that are worthy of maintenance in the future we must set out to create. There is much in our recent past and our present that will doubtless be contributory as we attempt to advance Jamaica Marketing Enterprise Inc. We simply need to be unusually discerning in our choices.

I do not believe that the general population of our country will have much difficulty discerning which aspects of our culture must be cast aside and which must be embraced. After all, the choices seem quite obvious to any observer who has been paying attention to the goings-on in Jamaica over the period since Independence. It should surprise no one that these choices will inevitably boil down to the known and acknowledged growth inhibitors, some of which were mentioned earlier: crime, deficiencies in education and training, lack of coherency in pursuing national policy and objectives, a political system that does not work in the interest of the people, unnecessary roadblocks set in place by an inefficient and at times indifferent bureaucracy, unwillingness to assess performance and hold those responsible accountable.

On this basis it should not be difficult to agree that there is some consensus on the diagnosis of our problem. There may not be such consensus when we come to proffer solutions.

PART THREE

THE CASE FOR RADICAL CHANGE

Never let your dreams reside in the

plans of another.

8

CHANGE AS AN IMPERATIVE

a. Rationale

Among a number of unavoidable questions raised at the outset is this crucial one: *Why do we not recognize the reality that unchanged behavior in the face of unchanging problems is most unlikely to bring about changed outcomes?* As a people, our response to this question will reveal our level of hostility to change or the extent to which we are aware of how inimical our uninterrupted commitment to the *status quo* has been to our progress. No thoughtful Jamaican at home or abroad can deny with any justification that change in our circumstances is not just necessary but imperative. This change runs the gamut from how we view performance and accountability through our approach to crime to our system of governance. Sadly, given the gravity of our dilemma, its duration and our ongoing acquiescence and complicity, it is entirely unacceptable, if not irrational, to believe or even hope that the continued application of palliatives to address our problems can possibly be effective.

An accumulation of detrimental issues makes it very difficult not to admit that as a nation we are at what is perhaps the most pivotal tipping point in our history. Circumstances such as ours are often described as a perfect storm for obvious reasons: our economy is in alarming decline; crime is eating away at the remnants of our nation's goodwill and the peace of mind of the entire population; political

131

malfeasance is taken for granted to such an extent that very few citizens bother to complain; our system of education, especially early childhood education, is in abject disarray; poverty has expanded its hold to the areas of mind and spirit. In short, the nation is now at serious risk of becoming a paradise completely lost.

I cannot envisage a traditional system or process by which our problems can be effectively addressed. The simple truth is that we have already tried all the typical prescriptions to no avail. A refill and reapplication of these topical remedies make little or no sense.

b. Direction

The path of change we seek cannot sensibly be seen as increased effort in the same direction in which we are currently headed. As indicated earlier, we seem to be on a circular route. We appear to have settled for a more restricted vision of our future than our Independence promised. It seems that we look back wistfully at our past and long for the good old days when we were all our neighbors' keepers, when respect for one another was universal, when crime was rare and laws were deeply respected, when parents never had reason to fear for the safety of their children, when being poor was never seen as justification for criminality, when the connection of violence and politics was at worst tangential and when social mobility was opportunity that beckoned the underclass to a future that was distinctly pregnant with the greatest of prospects. Regrettably, we are focused on a view from the rear view mirror of our lives rather than the view through the windscreen of our lives. There is a reason the windscreen is several times the size of the rearview mirror. We need to focus on the way ahead not the road behind us.

In order to maintain forward focus we must commit to a shared vision. Fortunately **Vision 2030 Jamaica** qualifies on this account even without the adjustments suggested earlier in our review of this plan. It is fair to say that this offers us a starting point for moving ahead at a time in our country when such a starting point could never be more necessary. Happily, all is not rotten in our island paradise. Indeed, we can now easily agree that we have a point of reference in our past, are fully aware of our current predicament and have a vision of our future that should be acceptable to the vast majority of us. However, before we may move ahead without reservations, there are contradictions in our environment and circumstances that we must acknowledge and address. Many of us may not see these as contradictions. After all, we have managed to do a most remarkable thing: we have effectively lived with these contradictions with a normalcy that is nothing short of astounding. In this respect these contradictions may become evident only after they have been explained. Still, the greatest contradiction of all is the frequent claim and explanation that a system that oppressed us as a matter of state policy is also the major driving force with the greatest potential for our effective liberation: Capitalism driven Democracy.

c. Colossal Contradictions

Our long embrace of traditional two-party-system-democracy validates our extraordinarily strong commitment to this model of governance. In fact, Jamaica's political stability is most often credited to our unquestionable adherence to the model. Generally, we take Democracy at face value and never question its bona fides as the most humanistic model of governance ever contrived by man. I suspect that we do not understand that this model is more than anything else an instrument of a much less humanistic scheme: Capitalism. While the linkage may not surprise us, the extent of the guidance and control of the latter over the other more than likely will. It is not unreasonable to contend that two-party-system-democracy is the very vulnerable ward of a plutocratic, oligarchy-sensitive, dysfunctional single parent generally known as Capitalism.

We need not look very far in order to see examples of the demonstrated deference to and protection of Capitalism at the expense of Democracy. There is no better place to observe the vexing reality than the United States of America. As I write there are cities in the state of Michigan, for example, that have been sequestered by the state's governor under a new law that puts these cities under the care of an appointed *emergency manager*. This manager is in effect a despot put in place by

a democratically elected governor. The emergency manager wields all of the powers attendant to his status as a despot except for the ability to raise taxes (an interesting exception that I suspect is meant to protect the wealthy against the unlikely
possibility). This new city ruler literally and legally replaces the entire elected city
council, including the mayor. The reason for this draconian intervention in the
city's governance is the determination by the state's governor that the city could
go bankrupt or default on certain identified liabilities. In other words, the choice
is clear: capitalist tenets trump our claimed commitment to democratic principles
such as the right of the people to govern themselves through those elected by the
electorate to govern. This remarkable inconsistency is now entrenched in the most
ardently acclaimed democracy in the world.

The superiority of capitalist requirements over traditional democratic
principles is even exemplified at a national level in America. The unresolved
debate over debt limits and deficit financing is a dramatic case in point. One
political party in the government is generally committed to ravaging programs
for the poor, children and the disabled, if not eliminating these entirely, in
order to satisfy what is claimed to be a fiscal dilemma so profoundly harmful to America's wellbeing that entrenched democratic principles are expend-
able in their address. This is the case although evidence clearly indicates that
the deficit is declining constantly and, by most accounts, cannot be claimed
with any convincing justification to be our primary problem at this time. In
fact, the majority of credible economists as well as the general public remains
convinced that the stubborn, high level of unemployment is the preeminent
problem for the U.S.

The abused filibuster convention mentioned earlier is among the means by
which approval of legitimate government funding is stymied. The main driving
force behind the unconscionable indifference to the most vulnerable in society
and the radical restrictions on government expenditure is the horrifying desire
to ensure the undisturbed wholeness of the major capitalist bastions in America's
free enterprise economy in which just 1% of the population owns 40% of the
country's assets. Do not lose sight of the fact that this is happening in the world's

most admired Democracy and the most aggressive international champion of the claimed exceptional virtues of this system.

Much more cynical and insidious is the incomprehensible response of the National Rifle Association (NRA) and its minions to the December 29, 2013 massacre of twenty children and six teachers at the Sandy Hook elementary school in the state of Connecticut. The reaction of 90% of the national population to this horror was the expressed desire for the implementation of restrictions that would reduce the likelihood that criminals or the mentally impaired could purchase military-style assault rifles as well as limit the size of high-capacity magazines that enable the killing of dozens of people in less than a few minutes. Yet, thirteen members of Congress in knee jerk support of the NRA and gun manufacturers decided to filibuster any legislation in keeping with what the majority of citizens demanded. To make assurance doubly sure this small group is even threatening not to allow any gun control measure to be brought before the Congress even for debate, let alone for a vote. In other words, a very small minority of the people's representatives was able to prevent even a debate on a matter of national significance. Is this Democracy?

At the heart of this incredible contradiction and inconceivable defiance is the motive of the NRA: to ensure that the sale of guns is never interrupted or made more difficult. In short, Democracy must be subject to the whims of capitalist greed and control. This is in total disregard for the principles of Democracy and incredible indifference to the massacre and the pain being endured by the parents of the slain children. The shamelessness of this maneuver is made worse by the absolutely discredited claim that any relevant firearms control legislation violates the 2nd Amendment to the Constitution of the United States of America. Nothing could be farther from the truth since the legislation that was being sought did not in any way prevent the people from purchasing or bearing arms; it sought solely, simply and explicitly to limit the type of arms and the capacity of ammunition clips to which the average citizen may freely have access. The fact that this deception was marketed as effectively as it was should leave the thoughtful in a state of bewilderment.

Given all this, how does Jamaica's similarly capitalism directed democracy fair? According to the report, **Regional Economic Outlook, Western Hemisphere: Shifting Winds, New Policy Challenges,** in comparison with 23 regional neighbors, Jamaica has the second-highest unemployment rate at roughly 12 per cent, and the fourth-highest poverty rate at about 43 per cent. Alarmingly, Haiti's poverty score in this report is better than that of Jamaica although Haiti is supposedly the poorest country in the Americas. It is also true that those who earn the most are least likely to pay the taxes they should. Of course, like the U.S.A. but to a much greater extent, we are facing a debilitating debt dilemma. Like the U.S.A., the preferred approach is to apply prescribed capitalist solutions that involve traditional approaches that disproportionately affect the most vulnerable in the society in spite of overwhelming evidence that these traditional approaches do not work. In a sense, there is not a great difference between IMF management and management by the city despot in Michigan. Regrettably, the results will likely be very similar in consequence. It is frighteningly instructive and ironic that the purposeful capitalist intervention protocol is seen as having the greatest potential for overcoming the failings of the democratic system of governance.

Given the universally extolled virtues and assumed effectiveness of Capitalism along with its anticipated superior outcomes, it seems only natural to wonder why it is that the capitalist model of management is not applied outright, at least in its essential characteristics, to state or national government. By this I mean the application of a centralized hierarchical system similar to that in place in every well run corporation with a CEO and board of directors. Such an arrangement is unitarian in nature and, in the final analysis, decidedly non-adversarial. Even when corporate board members may disagree with approaches or decisions, they suppress their dissent in deference to the will of the leadership and in the agreed best interest of the enterprise. Paradoxically, the democratic system itself does not disallow the free selection of such an arrangement. Keep this in mind as we proceed.

It is therefore deceitful to claim that we believe in and are deeply committed to democratic principles as, fundamentally, the ultimate means of governing, while simultaneously deferring to strictly capitalist principles when our Democracy runs into difficulty. Logically, this implies that capitalist objectives take precedence over democratic ones. In fact, even purely political preferences also trump democratic principles. We only need recall the about-face during the George Bush presidency in 2006 when peaceful, democratic elections in the Palestinian West Bank resulted in the election of Hamas, a group that America had declared terrorist. American and Israeli leadership subsequently reversed themselves in regard to their stated willingness to accept the election results and to work with the winner. The outcome did not meet either their expectations or preferences and hence was unacceptable. Undeniably, Democracy is therefore simply a means to a desired end and may be capriciously pushed aside if deemed necessary. In our case, as well as that of America, the end is free market security even when this serves predominantly or solely the interests of a minority. Democracy is reduced to simply being the means by which this end is achieved.

Less transnational in nature but similarly contradictory in character is the behavior of the Jamaican Diaspora when compared to the behavior of Jamaicans at home. The Diaspora's astonishing discipline, reluctance or downright refusal to accept failure and its notable willingness to conform to the rules of the road in foreign lands are starkly contrary to the behavior of its countrymen at home. It is highly debatable, of course, whether the members of the Diaspora would comport themselves similarly had they remained at home. There is no way to win such an argument. For the purpose of our endeavor it is only necessary to admit to the reality. So how do we explain this domicile sensitive deviation?

Jamaicans, like all other Third World immigrants, appear to migrate to First World countries for a single overwhelming reason: opportunity. It is fair to assume that where there is recognition of personal opportunity there is personal vision. Where there is personal vision there is a perception of how one sees oneself in the future. There is a preponderance of positive expectations. Perhaps the most limiting aspect of remaining at home is the unfortunate reality that opportunity is dramatically limited and hence severely restrictive of all the normally accompanying expectations. Even so, Jamaicans at home generally attempt to compensate for this clear limitation imposed by their circumstances. This is certainly more readily discernible among the more than 40% of the local population that, in common parlance, *hustle* to make a living or simply to make ends meet. Often enough this hustling is indifferent to the formal rules of trade and commerce and may even be illegal at times. In truth, hustling does require its own kind of smarts and discipline; it is just that these particular qualities now respond naturally to survival instincts rather than straightforward opportunity.

Over time, this hustling leads inevitably to a permanent resignation to circumstances that are admitted to be insurmountable, but only for the hustler, never for his children. In fact, the overriding justification for hustling is a sense that, while stuck in place, the hustler through his efforts sees some promise of opportunity beyond mere survival for his children. There are innumerable stories of Jamaicans at home that confirm the effectiveness of this survival strategy. As we should expect, however, there comes a time when some hustlers give up on the strategy out of sheer frustration and the realization that their expectations of opportunity for the next generation are unlikely to be met. This is the birth of hopelessness. We need to understand that there is nothing more menacing to the future of a nation than hopelessness among any large group of its citizens. This is precisely why there should be universal concern about the prolonged resignation of *sufferers*. This sense of hopelessness is also, incidentally, the reason for the apparently globally sensitive, endless conflict between the Israelis and Palestinians and the recourse to the tactics of terror by disaffected groups of radicals.

Luckily, in our case emigration provides a safety valve for many as a reliable exit from the debilitating malaise of hopelessness. Still, it cannot solve the problem and is at best no more than palliative. In the final analysis, the only effective, long-term solution is the creation of a national economy that serves the welfare of the majority of the people as well as validates their personhood. Even as we extol the virtues of two-party-system-democracy, its failure to arrive at this solution over 50 years of Independence has to be seen as disheartening at best and, at worst, hopeless. The story of a young Jamaican I met at the funeral of a friend in Tampa, Florida, not too long ago substantiates the point.

He was in his late-thirties to early-forties and reminded me of one of my own sons. He had migrated less than two years earlier. He had operated a small business near the docks in Kingston. Over time, small groups of idlers would greet him each morning on his arrival at his place of business. They asked for financial assistance nearly every day. More often than not he complied with their request but became very concerned that expectation of assistance had become permanent. Soon it was suggested to him that he needed protection to ensure the safety of his business and property. This is a common device in Jamaica, not only to secure an income stream for the protectors but to guarantee its permanency. Understandably, this escalation in fund-raising was seen eventually as threatening. The young man became afraid for his personal safety and made sure that he was never at his place of business too late in the evenings. This, together with the pervasive lawlessness in society at large, his concerns about the education of his young children and the bribes he paid to expedite the processing of documents at a number of government agencies, made him decide that his situation was hopeless. Unfortunately, this young man's experience is repeated all too often in Jamaica and is the trigger for yet another exodus of large numbers of young people, entrepreneurs and professionals from Jamaica. It is an exodus the country cannot afford.

No less alarming and potentially destructive of our future is the conclusion of a young, former politician who had served two terms in parliament; one in opposition and the other in government. In a discussion with him about my intention to write this book, he bluntly indicated that my ideas on how to change the political system in Jamaica in a bid to change the trajectory of our politics, and hence our country, were *idealistic* and unlikely to yield any meaningful results. His feeling is that once a political party had attained power it was unlikely to share it. Based on my knowledge of him and his experience, I know that he was not being dismissive but respectfully honest. Sadly, he indicated that, in his view, the massive bureaucracy in Jamaica, the slow pace at which government moved, the unwillingness of the people, collectively, to make short-term sacrifices for long-term gains, and the fact that, in most instances, the best interests of the country would be seen as secondary to party political considerations, made him conclude that although there is hope for Jamaica to change over a very long period of time, his best option on how to use his time was to focus his attention on the survival of his own family unit and to do the best he could for the people in his employ. In his view, politics in Jamaica was unlikely to retain the best people in the system as most who remain in politics would, in the long term, come under immense pressure to compromise their morals, values and attitudes in order to deal with the political realities of maintaining the political power they had acquired.

Unlike the previous example, this young Jamaican refuses to migrate. Fortunately, there is more than a single way in which to respond to the hopelessness seen by many in Jamaica; many will migrate, but many will remain. In either case, most continue to stay engaged in spite of their profound concern about their personal welfare and the future of their country.

In the face of all this, engrained in the psyche of the Jamaican immigrant is the absolute belief, perhaps not unrelated to the *hustle* mentality, that there is always a way to succeed, to get to the objective being sought. This mentality is of inestimable value in First World environments where opportunity is relatively abundant in the eyes of the immigrant. The fact that nothing succeeds like success simply provides a multiplier effect to the efforts and expectations of the immigrant. With this in mind, in the immigrant's adopted country, seen in somewhat religious terms as the Promised Land, failure is contemplated as no more than a remote possibility.

Individual response behavior is less complex and more easily explained than group response behavior, especially where the groups are dispersed and varied in status. For example, just as is the case with the host country's population, the Diaspora reflects variation in levels of education and training, employment and income, housing and visible standard of living. Nevertheless, the group response to basic laws such as traffic regulations, for example, is universal compliance. This is never the case at home in Jamaica where behavior on this account continues to get progressively worse. This atypical, universal compliance regarding rules and regulations in the host country is explained on two grounds: the first is the fact that in the new environment of the host country non-compliance is certainly the exception and not the rule; the second is that violations are immediately recognized and summarily punished. In a word, rules are enforced and violations addressed with remarkable certainty and consistency. In the host country the laws are generally respected whether the offender is a beggar or a billionaire. No one may reasonably claim that this is the case in Jamaica.

Now that we have some clarity on the contradictory nature of some major aspects of our circumstances on both the national and individual levels, we are in a better position to address the matter of change in Jamaica. The profile of the Diaspora and its relationship with Jamaica will provide a most stimulating point of reference in our attempt to show that favorable change is not only an imperative but a distinct possibility.

d. Change Agents

Much change occurs routinely in our national and individual lives with or without our guidance or direction. There can be no doubt that our direct and constant involvement with the phenomenon on a selective basis is advantageous. In order to make the best of our engagement we must be willing to examine all partnerships with potential to contribute favorably to the critical changes we seek. Remember, not only are we generally resource poor but unceasingly brain-drain inclined. We must be willing to see leadership in an unfettered, non-traditional manner. In order to facilitate this departure from the traditional we must refuse to be held hostage by the instinctive compulsion to confuse the nature of leadership with the nature of the enterprise that is being led or managed. In other words, we must be willing to observe leadership in the raw. On this basis, I contend that effective, successful leadership of an illicit enterprise is in principle identical in nature to that applied in a traditional, lawful enterprise. Not only does this perspective enlarge the pool of potential partners, it also reflects the recognition of our profound deficit in effective traditional leadership, a critical necessity given our circumstances. Especially under current conditions, every ounce of Jamaica's talent matters!

Even as we abhor the rampant crime and corruption in Jamaican society and find the scourge absolutely disgraceful and a threat to our future, there is no denying the evidence that garrisons are effectively organized and managed. By and large they serve the most basic survival needs of residents, demonstrate some semblance of concern and goodwill for the integrity of the community and ensure respect for and compliance with the rules that ensure the community's functioning and survival. This is not a glorification of garrisons but simply a detached, rational recognition of their functionality. It is not at all an idle exercise to compare the effectiveness of garrisons to that of the national government. Upon examination one may find it difficult to decide which of the two is more functionally effective.

It is perfectly understandable that the comparison may be seen by many as odious or repulsive, especially when the elements of violence and coercion are taken into account. I would quickly caution, however, that there is abundant evidence of the national government applying similar means, almost exclusively against the poor, of course, in its punitive attempts to enforce compliance with its wishes. It is also worth taking the time to contemplate just how tranquilizing and apparently natural has been our willingness to forgive and in some instances forget, it seems, the grave sins of our enslavers. We ought to be absolutely dumbfounded at the monstrous contradiction implicit in the observation. Is it simply that it is easier or more comfortable to forgive the teacher than to forgive the student? After all, our sordid history of violence, selective patriotism and predatory politics can be traced directly to the bitter roots of slavery and its aftermath.

The most illuminating explanation of the commonality of the predatory nature of power in Jamaican society is provided by Obika Gray in his absolutely remarkable work mentioned earlier, **Demeaned But Empowered:** *The Social Power of the Urban Poor in Jamaica*. To read Gray's work is to understand a most crucial fact about the nature of the relationship between politics and the poor and exploited, and how this group eventually jettisons its dependency on its political masters to become its own substantial agent via what Gray identifies in typically creative Jamaicanese as *badness-honour*. In this manner, the erstwhile poor and exploited, as a circumstantially cohesive group, have become the exploiter and manipulator of the once singular force of politics in Jamaica. A quote from Chapter 5, *Badness-Honour and the Invigorated Authority of the Urban Poor,* further clarifies this startling turn of events:

142

By 1971 badness-honour as a cultural practice had won moral dominance within the society of the Kingston poor. There a stylized outlawry ("badness" or "badmanism" in Jamaican parlance) provoked fear in the larger society but earned raves in the slums for challenging the norm of civility and for affirming a racially charged defiance as a new basis for social identity and honour. (p. 123)

As I indicated earlier, the songs and stories of the people are significant reflections of popular sentiment. In a footnote, Gray alludes to the Bob Marley song, *I Shot the Sheriff*, as a proclamation of the message and authority of the rebellious poor. Clearly, the new found power of the poor and marginalized is not only turned inward but represents an almost impregnable barrier against what used to be the frequent, casual, heavy handed incursions by the authorized agents of the coercive state.

Once we recognize leadership in the manner suggested earlier, we will be able to understand the nature and extent of the opportunity presented by sanitizing and coopting garrison leadership, for example, into what would become a reformed and most formidable association in an effective, relentless assault on the *status quo*. Regrettably, I am unable to recall the source of a commentary by a Jamaican professor at Harvard University in reference to the serendipitous part played by illegal pursuits early in the family history of some of the 400 most influential families in the United States of America. The professor justifiably contends that in a number of these cases the families were allowed to sanitize their illegally acquired wealth and deserved criminal reputation. This not only facilitated their acceptance into the ranks of the puritanical, tremendously influential gentry but permitted their continued accumulation of wealth in a manner that was now much more acceptable, significantly beneficial to the general welfare of the state as well as much more easily subject to institutional oversight. Clearly, all parties benefited greatly from this pragmatic accommodation. The professor suggests that this is an example that Jamaica should have considered in the case of Christopher Coke who appeared to have initiated steps to sanitize his unlawfully gained fortune along with his notorious reputation.

Many will see such an option as being without an iota of merit. Yet, history has a way of negating this contention. It has done so in the case of our colonial masters and in regard to America and its prohibition violators, for example. The intention of this accommodation is not that the state should become complicit in illegal activity. Rather, it is to make the best of a very egregious situation over which the state currently has little or no control, from which it does not benefit and that is severely harmful to the state and its residents. The state may even be seen as co-opted already through its corrupt leaders and agents. At the same time, both the state and the converted citizen stand to gain much from the bountiful benefits that most often accrue from such redemptive, pragmatic accommodation. In addition, and most importantly, the criminality that was the *raison d'être* of the now reformed citizen is permanently smothered.

Rightfully, the methodology of sanitization and co-optation should be of concern to all. I am certain that an entire volume could be written on the topic. For our purpose, however, a few suggestions will have to suffice in pursuit of what I believe to be a realistic path to redemptive, pragmatic accommodation and its likely benefits.

i. Truth & Reconciliation Process:

In circumstances such as those under discussion there would be great value in a truth and reconciliation exercise patterned after the iconic model initiated by the Republic of South Africa. Two quotes from Desmond Tutu provide the best guidance of all:

> *Without forgiveness there is no future.*

> *Forgiving is not forgetting; it's actually remembering — remembering and not using your right to hit back. It's a second chance for a new beginning. And the remembering part is particularly important. Especially if you don't want to repeat what happened.*

The case has already been made that there should be no point of difference between crime and corruption. The known corrupt members of the gentry will also be obliged to participate in the truth and reconciliation process. No deference can be shown to those who have traditionally been protected from the consequences of their crimes. And both victim and victimizer must participate.

ii. Verification of Assets:

All assets of the culpable must be verified and appropriate liabilities, including taxes, assessed and settled.

iii. Obligations of the Redeemed:

There will be a clearly defined path to redemption which all participants must formally commit to follow. This will include exposure to the formal operating structure, rules and obligations of legitimate business; all subsequent activities must conform to all pertinent laws and regulations; a period of probation will apply during which community service will be assigned; any violation of the conditions of probation will result in summary prosecution.

iv. Treatment of Victims:

Whether individual or institutional, e.g. government or its agents, victims will be verified, acknowledged and compensated from the funds of the redeemed where compensation is justified and feasible.

v. Documentation:

The process will be documented in its entirety and will be available to the public and institutions of higher learning with the prime intent being to create an institutionalized memory that will enhance the likelihood that the experience of wholesale criminal assault on Jamaican society will never have to be endured in the future.

The imperfection of the process is admitted, as is the expectation and hope that many will suggest worthwhile improvements. Still, the overwhelmingly critical aspect of all this is that we engage in a process of reconciliation that will, at a minimum, ensure a viable, new beginning toward a much more promising and reliable future.

Of course, we cannot overlook the less controversial partnerships that abound even as we recognize that these are much more readily and easily engaged. In fact, many are currently involved in attempts to mitigate the effects of crime with the intent to eliminate crime altogether from our society over time. Although acknowledged and praiseworthy, their degree of success is subdued and marginal though often achieved at great cost. These partners, nevertheless, should not be ignored; neither must their contribution and effort be shortchanged. In this regard we must develop an inventory of partners that will bridge the gap between traditional partnerships and the obviously non-traditional, admittedly controversial partnerships introduced here. This is crucial to our chances of success in achieving our objectives.

Needless to say, we cannot afford to ignore or alienate even a single one of our traditional partners in the fight against crime or in the support of efforts to improve the quality of leadership in the nation. Individuals as well as institutions must be targeted and engaged on a formalized, permanent basis by our current national leadership class, organized and directed with a single objective in mind: to make our society whole. Religious institutions, service clubs, athletic clubs, chambers of commerce, children's organizations such as the Boys' Scouts and Girls' Guides, schools, colleges and universities must all play a part in this complex nation saving endeavor. So demanding a task is this that it has to be at its core an all-hands-on-deck partnership if we are to have a better than average chance of beating the odds. The challenge is unlike any we have ever faced and is definitely not for the faint of heart. Hopefully, the effort we will make will ensure our fair share of luck, the intangible but necessary ingredient for success on adventures such as the one upon which we are about to embark.

e. Making the Sale

We have been on an unusual journey that encompassed vital areas of our past, alarming aspects of our present and dreadful anxieties about our future. Surely, we understand the inescapable linkages embedded in the reality. What must be understood with even greater intensity and purpose is our responsibility for the shaping of our future in keeping with the vision we must all take to heart: **Jamaica, The Place of Choice to Live, Work, Raise Families, and do Business**. In my view, fully half of our challenge lies in trusting this vision. We must believe! And we must not lose faith in hope. We must not succumb to despair when timelines in our plans are not met or when naysayers abound. We must hold steadfast to the realization that as long as progress is being made toward our objectives some delays are tolerable and likely inevitable in the scheme of things. What is intolerable is lack of progress or reversal of gains. We must also be realistic and smart regarding the priorities we choose to address at the start.

It is quite revealing that the number of Jamaicans returning home to retire has been in dramatic decline. *Over the last 20 years, the annual number of "returning nationals" has dropped by more than half — down to slightly more than 1,000 in 2011*; so states the e-magazine **Jamlink – Jamaica Matters** in a recent edition. This decline strikes directly at the very heart of the segment of the vision that declares Jamaica the place of choice to live. Returning nationals and Diaspora remittances most certainly account for at least a quarter of our foreign exchange earnings. There can be no doubt that serious disruption in this inflow will be extremely harmful to our ability to achieve our vision.

As indicated earlier, our plans will require adjustments as we move forward because of the natural fluidity of our circumstances. Our ability and willingness to make such adjustments will be critical to our continued progress. On this account it should be easily understood why it is imperative that we remain focused on our vision; it is the North Star on our journey. With this in mind there is every reason to hope that as we move to the next stage of our discussion we will not be so intimidated by the unusual nature of what is being proposed that we close our minds to possibility, promise and reason.

We must refer once again to the most telling question asked of ourselves so far: *Why do we not recognize the reality that unchanged behavior in the face of unchanging problems is most unlikely to bring about changed outcomes?* It is a question that is asked more often than many may be willing to admit. It may be that its frequency is indicative of the fact that it is seldom answered or answered in a manner that does not forthrightly confront the *status quo*. We have not only attempted to provide an answer to the question but will now bravely present a framework for a clearly different approach in response to our universally known and acknowledged intractable problems. The approach will certainly challenge the best in us as well as the best among us.

PART FOUR

THE RUBBER MEETS THE ROAD

When we embrace the evening of our lives

the night is unlikely to frighten us.

9

A FRAMEWORK FOR RADICAL CHANGE

Earlier I mentioned the hubris of those who claim the unique superiority of traditional Democracy over all other forms of government. It is comforting to note that I am not alone in the view that this contention is becoming not simply archaic but nonsensical in the face of overwhelming evidence to the contrary. In his new book, **No One's World:** *The West, the Rising Rest, and the Coming Global Turn*, Charles A. Kupchan, political scientist and Georgetown University professor, makes the telling point that it is quite clear that....*The world is headed toward multiple versions of modernity, not political homogeneity.* Democracy is constantly losing much of its luster as it demonstrates its inherent weakness in dealing with the pervasive issues of income disparity, corruption and manipulation by the wealthy. By its very tenets we should reasonably expect to see democracy-directed capitalism. Instead, we are witnessing the most blatant demonstrations of capitalism-directed democracy in both Europe and the United States in response to an unusually disruptive and extended global recession.

In May of this year **The Transatlantic Academy** mentioned earlier, a global partnership of think tanks led by the German Marshall Fund of the

United States, issued a benchmark report on the state of Democracy. Its title, **The Democratic Disconnect,** is as appropriate under the circumstances as any title could be.

> *"Democracy is in trouble," the report begins. "The collective engagement of a concerned citizenry for the public good — the bedrock of a healthy democracy — is eroding. Democratic governments often seem crippled in their capacity to deliver what their people want and need. They are neither as responsive nor as accountable as they need to be in an era of hard choices and rising nondemocratic powers. There is widespread concern about apparent declining rates of voter participation and about the alien- ation or disaffection of citizens from the political process."*

This report should be mandatory reading for every supporter or avowed lover of Democracy. Without a doubt it reflects a reality as well as a currency that con- tinues to be overshadowed by the fanatical commitment of those who believe in Democracy with religious zeal. All admirers and lovers of Democracy discredit or ignore this invaluable report at their peril.

Perhaps the most impressive example of alternative and effective governance is the approach being taken by the Chinese. We have already noted the Singaporean model to good effect. As Kupchan points out, the authoritarian government of China has managed to create a growing middle class that participates fully in the economic success of the country and is therefore unlikely to challenge Communist Party control. Even more telling is the fact that, according to a **Der Spiegel** review of Kupchan's book....*Some 80 percent of respondents to a survey in China said that they were satisfied with the country's direction, compared to less than 30 percent of respondents to a similar survey in the United States.* The evidence supports Kupchan's contention that the world is not becoming more homogeneous or more American but more diverse and less American. In fact, the growing internal diversity of the American population mirrors this change; a change that traditional America itself is finding quite discomforting and with which America continues to grapple with varying degrees of success and failure. The *status quo* appears to be making its last stand as it attempts to fend off the inevitable.

It is particularly instructive that we consider Kupchan's listing of the top five economies as they appeared in 2010 versus how they will likely appear by 2050.

The 2010 list:
1. The United States of America
2. China
3. Japan
4. Germany
5. France

The 2050 list:
1. China
2. The United States of America
3. India
4. Brazil
5. Russia

The transformation is undeniably dramatic as Japan, Germany and France bite the dust and the number 1 and 2 countries change positions.

All of this should encourage some realization among Jamaicans that the sanctity with which we view our traditional two-party-system-democracy is unwarranted. There can be no doubt that the time has come for an honest review of our system of governance with a view to embracing a new, more honest and more humanistic pragmatism in the management of our affairs. In this regard, we need to pay attention to the intent and actions of the group of countries identified as BRICS – Brazil, Russia, India, China, and lately, South Africa (a recent addition). In the **guardian. co.uk** of April 2, 2013 we learn from contributor Radhika Desai that these countries have laid the foundation for a development bank that should rival the IMF and World Bank. Naturally, this is being met, not surprisingly, with what Desai calls the *usual* *western skepticism.* Nevertheless, she points out that, unlike previous similar arrangements, this action actually puts in place steps to create an institution as well as a Contingent Reserve Agreement to pool reserves with initial inputs of $41bn from China, $18bn each from Brazil, India and Russia and $5bn from South Africa. Desai is convinced that....*Not since the days of the Non-Aligned Movement and its demand for a New International Economic Order in the 1970s has the world seen such a coordinated challenge to western supremacy in the world economy from developing countries.* In keeping with Kupchan's observation, this could be a palpable sign of the new multipolarity of the new world order. The *status quo* is under assault and for good reason.

A. The Outline of a Plan

The entire purpose of the preceding chapters is to prepare the reader for what the following discussions will propose. If the effort was successful we should be able to contemplate the upcoming arguments with some equanimity and willingness to imagine a new beginning as well as a more hopeful future for ourselves and our country. The *status quo* and its constancy as a deceiving comforter have been examined and candidly scrutinized, criticized and exposed. It is hoped that by this point we have become significantly less susceptible to its wiles and our own fear of change.

In principle, we must acknowledge that only radical change can slow, end and reverse Jamaica's frightening decline towards failure as an exemplary, viable nation. We must also acknowledge that the time frame in which this change may be meaningfully implemented is not indefinitely elastic. The overriding objective cannot be unclear or misunderstood. Simply stated, it is to make Jamaica whole as a nation and to ensure the visibly virtuous functioning of the government and its agents. If this objective is achieved all other agencies of social significance, especially in the private sector, will benefit automatically. There can be no doubt that an effectively virtuous, functioning government will have profoundly positive impact on all areas of Jamaican society. As we proceed we must constantly keep in mind the priorities set out earlier. These, you may recall, are based on **Vision 2030 Jamaica**.

In addition, let me be clear: there is no intention to provide the definitive details of how we will arrive at agreement on the mechanics of the process being outlined. This discussion is what it says it is – merely an outline of possibilities that will hopefully stimulate new thinking and provide some initial guidance as to an alternative direction we should very seriously consider pursuing. Just in case our leaders prematurely decide that what is being proposed is not merely unworthy of consideration but impossible, I strongly suggest they pay attention to the ongoing attempts by the young President of Mexico, Enrique Peña Nieto, to transform Mexico's politics, challenge the most powerful and abusive among Mexico's elite and directly attack the scourge of crime. In other words, frontally attack the *status quo*. Already Nieto has initiated bold reforms and signed a *Pact for Mexico* with the two opposition parties. The title of the reform paper, *Pact for Mexico*, is most noteworthy. In an article, ***Working through a reform agenda*, The Economist** of April 6, 2013 makes the following observation:

> *Behind these reforms lies a "Pact for Mexico" struck between the PRI and the two main opposition parties in December. The Pact unites Mexico's political parties against the unelected interests that have long defied them. As he signed the Pact on behalf of the left-wing Party of the Democratic Revolution (PRD), Jesús Zambrano declared that politicians were "outraged that de facto powers of all kinds have time and again broken governments of one party or another."*

Clearly, all political parties are convinced that after far too many years of inaction and corrupt governments it is time to put the country first in order to solve Mexico's debilitating problems. The case of Mexico is even worse than Jamaica's in the sense that one political party, the PRI, ran the country for seventy continuous years until the year 2000. It may surprise many to know that the PRI is also the party of the current President. Positive change is not impossible. It requires foresight and courage.

i. First Steps

A nucleus of true and committed patriots from both political parties and civil society numbering no more than fifteen in all will be the arrowhead of the vector of change being proposed: ten parliamentarians including the Prime Minister (PM) and leader of the opposition (LOP) along with five representatives from non-government organizations (NGO). This group must set about agreeing to the intent, process and outcomes of what is being proposed here. The very basic initial step is to convince MPs and the nation that the time has come to put the country first, unequivocally. Realistically, only the Prime Minister can credibly initiate this process. This requires submerging traditional personal and party political ideology and senseless hypocrisy in deference to the obviously larger obligation of rescuing our country that is in unquestionably deep distress. This agreement will be put in writing, signed by every member of this group, notarized and publicly displayed in parliament and around the country. The work being done by the members of this group will not be compensated. If this endeavor is not strictly a labor of love, then we may as well agree that our situation is truly hopeless and abandon this pursuit of viable solutions to our problems.

The PM, the LOP and one member of the NGO group selected by agreement between the PM and LOP, will be equal partners in leading the Group of 15 (G-15). Every decision made by this tripartite leadership team must be unanimous. Any public display of disagreement among this leadership team will result in the summary removal and replacement of the guilty party, except where the guilty party is the P.M. or LOP. In this case he/she will be publicly censored by the rest of the G-15 on the basis of the three-strikes-and-you-are-out baseball rule. In this ultimate case, the G-15 will be automatically disbanded and we will admit to failure and hopelessness.

There is no doubt that the challenge as well as the opportunity presented here is as unique in our political history as it is uniquely difficult. The G-15 arrangement provides a laboratory for learning and testing regarding the nature of the process that will be pursued on a larger scale when the entire government becomes united and engaged in what is essentially a profoundly transformational exercise. The best way to understand this process is to explain that it is the purposeful change of the mindset among those who are designated as leaders, from an inherent predisposition to politicize and grandstand to a distinctly principled preference to cooperate and lead. This change is nowhere more urgently required than in the person of the Prime Minister.

This kind of leadership, out of sheer necessity if nothing else, must start at the level of the maximum leader in the government. Above all others, this person will be responsible for educating his/her political party, the government and the public at large on the process and the essential reasons for the timely transformation effort. This process, its intent and anticipated outcomes must be marketed to all Jamaicans at home and abroad with no less fervor and commitment than our leaders apply to electioneering. The G-15, in concert with the civil service or technocracy in its designated role, will draft all the necessary documents that will become the rules of play for the implementation of the proposed changes. It is anticipated that this process will require a period of no less than 3 - 5 years.

ii. Moving Against the *Status Quo*

There are a few critical things upon which we may agree: we are resource poor in money and management expertise and must anticipate yet another exodus of high-value citizens; the change we need and actively seek requires that we move beyond the traditional approaches routinely taken in the past to address our problems; we must be shrewd and courageous in our thinking and be willing to take reasonable risks in order to achieve our vision; we can ill afford politicization of the process being proposed; we must embrace unusual transparency within the G-15 and between the G-15 and the people at large; we must be honest with ourselves.

By now we should have come to accept that our continued deference to the *status quo* is extremely harmful to our prospects. Perhaps the most extensive and potentially harm-inducing aspect of the *status quo* is our continued wholesale adherence to a traditional, outdated, non-performing two-party-system-democracy. It has not served us well and there is no reason to believe that this reality is likely to change over time. If we truly believe this then we must act to modify or abandon the system altogether. The system is by design relentlessly competitive and adversarial. Such a system is unlikely to work well where there is widespread discrepancy in available information, education, opportunity for advancement, excessive levels of poverty and a dearth of virtuous leadership. In fact, our post-colonial experience unquestionably supports the greater likelihood of continued dysfunction on account of these inadequacies. Moreover, the abundant examples of similar dysfunction in far older, pre-eminent traditional democracies only serve to support the contention.

We may choose to remain yoked to the claim of a deceptively invaluable *loyal opposition* even though experience most often reveals this to be among the most persistent and pointless of oxymorons. It is natural that any group that is in opposition will remain more committed to its own welfare than to the welfare of the group that it legitimately opposes but with which it is traditionally and pretentiously expected to cooperate. In the future we need to be decidedly more focused on being cooperative than on being adversarial; being more pro-country than pro-party.

The process enshrined within the two-party-system-democracy has buried within it an institutionalized necessity to always seek out and exploit the failings or weaknesses of the opposing party and with scant regard for the harm this practice may inflict on the country whose interests both parties claim to serve unreservedly. The process also permits, if not outrightly encourages, exploitation by third-party interventionists within and without the country. Obviously, this diminishes the potential for effective governance and successful outcomes. Most regrettably, the system all but enshrines the distinctly partisan approach to the distribution of unavoidably limited and necessary government assistance to the poor who comprise the bulk of the population. On this basis, the party in power has very little incentive to pay attention to the plight of those who support the so-called loyal opposition. It should be no surprise to any observer that such a system, especially in so-called Third World countries, divides communities, marginalizes large numbers of citizens and breeds socially injurious enclaves such as garrisons.

iii. Constitutional Adjustments & Other Considerations

Provisionally forsaking the traditional two-party-system-democracy for a government of national unity must therefore be seen as a reasonable, viable option. Such a government is intended to foster unity of purpose and cooperation, deny automatic adversarial party culture and expressly discourage doctrinal, divisive, destructive political patronage. This is essentially a Unitarian system. This system will in all likelihood require amending our Constitution in spite of the fact that it is intended here for parliament to use the customary powers of the flawed traditional democratic process to authorize the dramatic transformation in how we are governed. This assumes, of course, that we have successfully executed the First Steps outlined earlier and now have a unified government that is fundamentally a coalition of the most worthy representatives from both political parties. Such success will powerfully exemplify extraordinary, united parliamentary leadership that will doubtlessly cause the region and the world to pay attention. The *new dispensation* will commence after the end of the parliamentary term during which parliament agrees to the changes being proposed.

The proposed system will be subject to a referendum if less than 60% of the current parliament agrees to move to a Unitarian form of government. A simple majority of the national electorate is all that will be required to authorize implementation of the Unitarian form of government. It is essential that the people are engaged, understand and buy into the proposed changes.

The Unitarian system being proposed is based on the following considerations, a number of which will surely require amendments to our cloned Westminster-style Constitution:

a. Duration – There is meaningful value in ensuring that the electorate understands that the system being proposed does not and will not claim to be the best of all possible systems. Any such claim is nonsensical. After all, we have roundly and justifiably denounced a similar claim by the purveyors of the traditional two-party-system-democracy. What may be claimed with justification, based on abundant evidence, is the fact that the traditional system has failed. On this account the proposed system will be provisional for a period of at least 50 years from commencement. At the end of this time, if deemed necessary, the people may freely choose any alternative system if they so desire, on the same basis as they freely furloughed the traditional system, to embrace the proposed Unitarian system. This is a pragmatic approach to our circumstances that offers the best chance to rescue our country from the travails of continued stagnation and decline. Undoubtedly, it will also attest to the extent to which we have matured as a people.

b. Parliamentary Representation – Given our financial state of affairs, the dearth of excellence in leadership and management expertise among our political class and the deep desire and need to be efficient, it is my view that parishes are over-represented in Parliament. Excessively high numbers of parliamentary representatives cannot compensate for indifference, incompetence or malfeasance.

The Jamaica House of Parliament has 63 members at an average of about 43,000 people per representative. In comparison, the U.S. House of Representatives has about 700,000 people per representative. The five states whose populations most closely match Jamaica's actually average 766,000 people per representative. In the U.K. the comparable ratio is about 90,000 people per representative. There is every reason to believe that parliament could, and perhaps should, function much more effectively were the number of representatives cut in half to no more than 31 members. On this basis, no parish will have more than two representatives. This proposed change will bring Jamaica's representation ratio to about 87,000 people per representative. While the 31 members include the position of Prime Minister, it should be noted that the Prime Minister will be elected separately from all other MPs under the system being proposed.

In addition, Parliament must not only execute its responsibilities but must appear to do so. Accordingly, Parliament should meet at least 50 times each year. In order to succeed at what is being proposed, no less than this degree of attention and executive effort will be required.

c. The Senate – I see no justifiable need for the 21-member senate. There is not a single discernible vital need that is served by its existence. To be charitable, its relevance and usefulness appear to be based wholly upon our inherited parliamentary tradition. Yet another example of how we have been *Westministerized*. To be brutally frank, its purpose appears to be to institutionalize sinecures for failed politicians and stalwart party loyalists. The elitist British House of Lords seems to be the essential model for this appendage of status, entitlement and political patronage. It should be roundly rejected as a model for the same reason we should reject the Monarchy. In short, the institution of the Senate should be discarded altogether.

d. The Governor General – We should agree to the timing for abandoning the position in favor of a ceremonial President as soon as we become a Republic. While we certainly cannot consider this a priority at this time, the step is a meaningful and useful one and should be planned for with much deliberation. Perhaps we will be in a position to implement this change at some point over the next 10 - 15 years.

e. MPs (excluding the PM) – All sitting MPs at the time of transition to the new Parliament will be eligible to compete in elections for the new Parliament under the new rules. In subsequent elections, no non-sitting candidate will be allowed to compete for a seat in Parliament unless such a candidate provides an authenticated list of names, corresponding signatures and addresses of at least 5% of the officially recognized electorate in support of his candidacy in the parish in question. The document for collecting such signatures will be the official, standard document provided by the office of the Commissioner of Elections. The authenticity of the data will be subject to validation by the Commissioner of Elections. Winning candidates must win at least 50% of votes cast or there will be a run-off between the candidates with the two highest numbers of votes.

f. The Position of Prime Minister – Under the Unitarian system the position of Prime Minister will be subject to a national vote. All candidates for the position should be the most visibly knowledgeable about and committed to the National Plan. The Prime Minister will now be required to be more of a chief executive, a manager and leader rather than a politician-in-chief. He will be obliged to convince the people of his knowledge of the National Plan and his ability to implement the Plan on a national scale. He must be unequivocally committed to the National Vision. The stated rules of funding detailed later will apply to the election campaign of all candidates for office, including those vying for the position of Prime Minister.

In order to prevent abuse at the time of the first election under the new system, no more than two candidates from each of the two major parties will be allowed to seek the office at the time of transition. If no candidate wins at least 50% of the votes cast, there will be a run-off between the candidates who received the two highest numbers of votes. In subsequent elections for the office of Prime Minister, non-serving candidates will qualify in the manner indicated above for MPs, except that candidates for the office of Prime Minister will have to secure an authenticated list of no less than 5% of the national electorate on a parish-by-parish basis. The Prime Minister is now beholden to the national electorate not to a political party or faction.

g. Campaign Platforms – Platforms will be based entirely on the National Plan. In this way every representative must win the support and trust of the people based on the extent to which he or she convinces the electorate of the value that the National Plan will add directly to the constituency. The politician will now be obliged to clearly understand and demonstrate his faith in and commitment to the National Plan. The focus of politics will become the selling and implementation of the National Plan and not the trite, non-specific and highly dubious claims and promises of traditional campaigning based purely on party platforms. In other words, the central concern of politics will now be leading and managing the country as a going enterprise rather than as a political minefield. In this manner there can be no hiding from performance against vision, plans and objectives. Neither can there be escape from accountability. This, in fact, will be the death knell of the *status quo*. There is no more worthy political objective than this.

h. Campaign Finance – All political campaigns will be overwhelmingly financed from the public purse. In the first instance the G-15 will decide on the amount to be allocated per qualified candidate. Subsequently, the decision will be the responsibility of the new Parliament. Total Funding from personal and all other sources may not exceed 30% of the agreed public funding amount. No campaigning or campaign financing may commence earlier than 6 months prior to any election.

Should there be unspent campaign funds in any election cycle all such funds must be remitted to the established Campaign Finance Fund. All such funds must be allocated to candidates in the following election cycle. Campaign funds may be used only for the purpose intended as stipulated in the applicable law. It will be a requirement that proper accounting be kept for all expenditures on this account. The Electoral Commission will be responsible for overseeing this regime. Violations will attract substantial penalties up to and including imprisonment.

i. Term Limits – The evidence confirms that length of service in Parliament does not correlate favorably with effectiveness or the quality of service provided by parliamentarians. In fact, it appears that there is an inverse relationship between length of service and positive contribution. Term limits are therefore an essential element of the proposed system. All MPs, except the Prime Minister, may serve no more than two terms of four years each whether these terms are consecutive or not. The Prime Minister will serve no more than two terms of five years each whether these terms are consecutive or not.

j. Protocol – There is a number of activities and processes whose importance requires particular identification. Many of these affect the very integrity of the proposed system. The ones considered most critical are identified and discussed below:

1. Partisan Politics: During the life of the Unitarian Parliament no member, including the PM, may publicly or privately campaign on a partisan basis. All campaigning must have as its focus the National Plan. In the event of a tied vote in the Parliament, the PM who is normally not allowed to vote will cast the deciding vote. Under clearly identified circumstances, e.g. incapacity of the PM, MPs will, by simple majority vote, elect one of their members to the position of Acting PM. The duration of the position will be limited to a maximum of one calendar year in addition to the time stipulated for the national election of a new PM should the PM be unable to return to active duty within the year. The new PM will then serve the normal term of 5 years.

2. The Civil Service and Parochial Support Systems: These may be adjusted to reflect the extent of the adjustment to Parliament. This adjustment should reflect the genuine need for technical expertise and local representation as justified from time to time by the complexity and urgency of the National Plan. This adjustment may be up or down based strictly on determined and agreed need. Such adjustments must be approved by a simple majority of those comprising the government.

3. Assessment/Update of the National Plan: The national government will be obliged to advance the National Plan continuously, with clear indication of priorities. Every four years this updated Plan must be placed before the electorate along with competing cost estimates and related time lines. This National Plan and performance against this Plan will be the basis on which government performance will be judged and elections contested.

4. Personal Assets and Liabilities: All persons elected to office must publicly declare all assets and liabilities and will not be permitted to invest in or benefit from any venture related to his/her office or any other government-related enterprise. All personal investments must be placed in a verifiable, de facto blind trust for as long as a Member of Parliament is in office. Naturally, this also applies to the Prime Minister. Severe penalties, including summary removal from office, a permanent ban from holding any political office, prosecution and imprisonment will apply to all convicted violators without exception.

5. Lobbying: No former holder of political office may engage in lobbying or consulting that directly involves interfacing with any political office holder or the government generally, within a period of five years after leaving office.

6. The Army, Agriculture and The Tourist Industry: This unusual linkage is a dramatic departure from the norm and holds immense promise for the country being finally able to feed itself from locally produced crops. This will significantly reduce local dependence on imported foodstuff as well as favorably impact the country's level of employment and its balance of payments.

It is immensely difficult to argue against the contention that the Jamaica Defense Force (JDF) serves little more than ceremonial purposes. Jamaica as a state has no known or even imagined enemies. It is therefore extremely unlikely that the island would ever be attacked or invaded. In any case, it is highly doubtful that we could effectively fend off such an attack. Our problems of security are absolutely internal and linked to political corruption, high unemployment, poor education, limited to no formal industrial training and general surrender to the scourge of crime. According to the April 15, 2013 edition of **Caribbean 360,** it is remarkable that two high-profile Jamaicans, the Minister of National Security, Peter Bunting, and the wife of the Governor General, Lady Allen, have simultaneously admitted to their frustration with our failure to reduce significantly the level of crime in Jamaica. We need to treat the root cause of the scourge and not continue to lament its symptoms. We must re-examine the traditional purpose of the armed forces and consider their as yet untapped potential as a real, positive game changer in our national life.

In my youth in Jamaica, every elementary school I knew and every prison of which I was aware had a garden or farm that produced enough food to feed large numbers of people. This was also the case with the Jamaica School of Agriculture. It is time that our army become involved with agriculture on a broad, national, commercial scale. This innovation would simultaneously address two related problems: praedial larceny that notably discourages commercial farming and the absorption of a large number of unemployed or underemployed young people.

Suitable government lands should be allocated for the purpose and a massive employment scheme initiated to employ thousands of young people who would be trained and supervised by the army on commercial size farms all over the country. Employment opportunities should be given first to the youth and especially those residing in the areas surrounding these farms. Where necessary, housing should be provided. Wages and benefits should amount to a reasonable living wage. This may mean exempting the income of these workers from taxes. This approach has the potential to transform our economy in meaningful and extensive ways when we consider obviously attractive linkages with entities like GraceKennedy, the Jamaica

Agricultural Society, the hotel industry and the Jamaica Tourist Board, for example. The first priority is to feed ourselves. The second priority is to satisfy no less than 90% of the food requirements of our hotels. The third priority is to prepare, package and export all surplus.

Understandably, there will be reservations concerning the linkage of our local agricultural output with our tourist industry. These reservations are not entirely baseless. However, they can be addressed intelligently to good effect. One notable fear is that tourists will find our potatoes, carrots, tomatoes, lettuce and other produce unattractive and less tasty than they would prefer. In other words, they do not look like or taste like typical, comparable North American produce. This is quite ironic since North American consumers are now paying significantly higher prices for what is called *organic* produce. By this is meant produce grown without the extensive use of chemicals or fertilizers or with only verifiable, minimal amounts of these. According to Caroline Scott-Thomas in the April 24, 2012 edition of **Food navigator-usa.com,** the market for organic foods in the U.S. grew by 9.5% in 2011 and broke the U.S. $30-billion barrier for the first time. Crops grown in Jamaica would automatically qualify on this score, naturally. Our problem is a lack of insight that prevents us from recognizing the advantage and opportunity this reality offers. We should lay claim to the naturalness of our foods and integrate this claim aggressively with the marketing of our tourist industry.

Still, should we feel obliged to make our produce look and taste more like North American produce, this presents yet another opportunity for linkage. The link between our agricultural endeavors and academic research to address this concern is patently obvious. We must begin to see this more as an opportunity than as a problem and develop strategies and plans to transform our thinking regarding what local hotels serve their guests. I have no delusions about the likely knee-jerk response of the major hoteliers to this approach. After all, it is infinitely easier and simpler to obtain an import license than to effectively support local agriculture. Undoubtedly, successive governments have been complicit in this shortsightedness. Change is never comfortable and is never without some risk. Yet, effective management should be expected to respond to this, not only as a worthy challenge to its competence and foresight, but also as an important contribution to the welfare of the nation. It goes without saying that political leadership has to be the catalyst in this innovative approach to a long standing problem.

While this strategy will necessarily be initiated by government, we should contemplate entering into critical, strategic shareholder partnerships with private enterprise at every level of this project. The hotel industry or its individual members, for example, should be wooed as essential partners in this regard. The expectation is that government will disinvest completely in the project eventually by selling its shares at market value after the project is up and running.

This project also has additional transformative potential that could be very effectively used to address crime, the national reform initiative involving the redemption of criminals as well as the sanitizing of their illicit gains. It is not without value that the eyes and ears of the security forces would be dispersed over large areas of the country for a protracted period. This should have a visible impact on crime. It is conceivable that the very management skills demonstrated by dons, for example, could have honest application here. Naturally, these skills would be exercised within the framework of the formalized, structured leadership and management regime of the enterprise and its management.

We should not be hesitant to ask for technical assistance from those most experienced and technically advanced in this type of farming endeavor. In the past, for example, we have been assisted by the Israelis in other aspects of farming. We may again need their assistance and should ask for this without compunction. It is difficult to imagine a more transformative project than the one under discussion.

7. The Triple 'A' Priority: We must immediately address the matter of crime. Given the unquestionable gravity of the situation, we literally have no choice in the matter. Our attempt must be different from all previous attempts. Above all, it will demand no less than exceptional leadership and will from the Prime Minister and Parliament. To recall our review of the opportunity missed by former Prime Minister Bruce Golding is to realize most painfully the absolute insufficiency of anything less.

Of course, there are no reliable statistics to determine or confirm the numbers of the criminal masterminds who continuously hold the society at large as well as the Diaspora hostage. Nevertheless, my guess is that they are unlikely to number in excess of a thousand to two thousand fearless, ruthless individuals. This assumption begs the question as to why, as a nation, we remain incapable of ending the scourge of criminality. We must confiscate every illegal firearm as a matter of the greatest urgency. Even if such an exercise requires house-to-house searches and curfews over several months, this must be done.

Laws must be passed and enforced making possession of any illegal firearm a felony that subjects the violator to summary detention without the possibility of bail and life imprisonment upon conviction. As an exercise of good faith and in preparation for the drastic steps that will be taken to address possession of illegal firearms, government should offer amnesty for a period of six months. During this time illegal firearms may be surrendered to the authorities at no risk. It may even be a worthwhile consideration to buy back these weapons from their illegal holders as an additional incentive. Thereafter the state must show no mercy to those who continue to violate the applicable laws. Those guilty of complicity must be treated in identical fashion.

No firearms are made in Jamaica. They must arrive there by air or sea. Technology exists to survey our coastline continuously as well as to monitor any shipments deemed to require the closest of scrutiny by government agents. There is no acceptable excuse not to address the issue of illegal firearms with every resource available and to do so with finality. Failure on this account guarantees failure at every other item in our list of priorities. I am unable to imagine any acceptable explanation or excuse for failure at this obligation.

The task at hand cannot be as difficult as many would have us believe. I once visited one of the small, rural towns in Jamaica some fifteen or more years ago with a friend who resided there. The landscape was visibly different from my earlier visits. Now there were numerous upscale residences perched impressively on the hillsides. In a few years prosperity had come to the little town. My friend indicated that this new prosperity was directly related to the drug trade. What was more telling is his confirmation that everyone in the community, including law enforcement, knew who the drug dealers were. These dealers were nevertheless left completely alone to operate openly without the slightest concern.

This little town is not unique. There can be no doubt that popular indifference and support as well as institutional tolerance of the type exemplified here may be witnessed all over the island. The authorities know who these miscreants are. This provides us with an initial advantage that should not be squandered, especially when it is an established fact that the trade in illegal firearms is directly related to the traffic in drugs. What has been missing so far in dealing with this problem is exceptional leadership along with the equivalent will on the part of local and national government. It should be considered treasonous for this state of affairs to be allowed to continue unaddressed.

B. Timing and The Pace of Change

These are critical aspects of any plan but much more so of the one under consideration. Not only do we move excessively slowly on all things but we are also demonstrably averse to change – even when the contemplated change is the exorcizing of evil.

In regard to timing, our tragic state of affairs eliminates any justifiable argument against urgency and immediacy. Immediate action is now mandatory. We must instantly take steps to address the most crucial priority of crime and corruption and simultaneously embark on the marketing of the overall plan to transform how our country works. While we must allow for a longer time horizon in regard to transforming how our country works, forceful action on crime and corruption must be taken immediately. Our thinking and action must reflect this urgency. We may be resource challenged but not to the extent that we are unable to address these two issues simultaneously. The greatest challenge relates to conviction and will on the part of the maximum leader and the general leadership class. The task is not only difficult but mandatory. Failure is not an option.

It is vital that, along with timeliness, we give due consideration to the pace at which we may reasonably expect to initiate the changes being pursued. There is no formula to determine a timeline but it would appear that a three to five year period is not an unreasonable initiation period. Any such expectation must be publicly acknowledged by government and regular reports made to the nation on progress. There must be no hesitancy to celebrate progress, just as there must be no reluctance to admit disappointment and to outline with clarity and conviction how any shortfalls will be addressed. We are involved in a war that we simply cannot afford to lose.

C. Implications for the Long Term

It should be obvious to all that the extent to which we fail or succeed at the transformation proposed here will determine the quality of life of individual citizens as much as it will define the place we may legitimately claim or hold among all or any group of countries: large or small, rich or poor, admired or reviled. We must be aware that the long-term may not be as long as we may like it to be. Indeed, as John Maynard Keynes famously noted, *in the long run we are all dead.* None should take this literally here but the reference is meaningful enough. Our failure to act decisively to address our problems will literally guarantee that we are dead to progress along with all its attendant benefits and abundant promises of a better future for all as a people and as a country.

The implications of failure or success, regardless of the side of the ledger on which we may eventually be scored, are equally consequential. While history clearly confirms our earlier misfortunes and exploitation, we dare not blame others for our inadequate response or our perverse adoption of the philosophy and practices of our oppressors. Even as we may allocate blame in retrospect, we must admit to our own complicity and insufficiency as we assess the journey we have made and the place at which we have arrived. Our future is our responsibility entirely. As horrendously harmful as our history has been to our early progress, it has surely taught us an invaluable lesson: we are accountable for our vision of ourselves as a people and as a nation, for the choices we make in response to the problems and challenges we face and for the successes and failures that inevitably arise from the actions we take. Not only did we demand our independence; we achieved it. Personal and national accountability attend this achievement. It is an obligation from which we cannot escape.

We were cautioned earlier about overcommitting to the *status quo*. The opposite caution is to be issued here. It is impossible to overcommit to our obligation to address our problems and secure our future. Such is the extent of the obligation of current leadership and the undeniable responsibility of the immediately succeeding generation. We ignore or fail to address this to our individual, collective and national peril.

10

APOLITICAL ENGAGEMENT FOR SUCCESS

a. Misreading the Signs

We have conveniently bought into the myth of the inevitable benevolence of our inherited, addictive, traditional Democracy. We have seen that there is nothing naturally endearing or culturally exemplary, let alone altruistically unique, about Democracy. The progress of China and Singapore strongly supports this contention. Examples of gross institutional disruptions, shameless insensitivity to the plight of the disadvantaged in deference to the welfare of the rich and clearly systemic societal failures in places like the United States, the United Kingdom, Greece and Spain in response to serious economic challenges only serve to strengthen the argument. Without a doubt, the naturally dysfunctional nature of purposefully adversarial multi-party politics simply makes a bad situation much worse. Traditional Democracy appears better at harnessing influence and power than at solving national problems. It certainly is more supportive of the welfare of the few than the welfare of the many despite its vociferous claims to the contrary. Worst of all, it seems that commitment to the *status quo* is built into its political DNA. It never achieves its promises and consistently fails to meet the expectations of those it so strongly pursues and converts into true believers.

This, in a nutshell, is the quintessential two-party-system-democracy politics into which we were totally immersed, first by our oppressors as willing, subservient converts and later by our own brethren as assertive, at times opportunistic, surrogates and hopeful partners in the enterprise of national Independence. The euphoria of being our own independent political agents overwhelmed our natural, self-preservation instincts honed during decades of servitude. Regrettably, we failed to be as cautious as we should have been about our new condition and our erstwhile oppressors. This new condition was so much better than any we had ever imagined that we neglected to observe that what should have created great discomfort among our former masters did nothing of the kind. This should have been a sign that our own future welfare was unlikely to be what our new condition signaled it to be. In fact, subsequent history reveals that, from the very beginning, our welfare was at risk.

The Lindsay-supported Fanon contention regarding the relationship between former oppressors and the oppressed does have resonance here. The former oppressed are unlikely to be completely vested in their own wellbeing if they take over the plantation, the great house, the wardrobe and the instruments of the former oppressor and at the same time permit the former oppressor to live comfortably and rent free in the guest house. We are all aware of how naturally deferential we always are to our guests. There are attendant costs to this conduct, not the least of which is the endless need to demonstrate our independence lest our constant deferential behavior be misunderstood by the people or misinterpreted by the former oppressor. It is a complex conundrum that all too often diverts our focus and redirects our energy from what must be, after all, our own primary and superior communal and political need: individual and collective wholeness or recovery from a purposely fractured existence.

The situation makes us very reluctant to rock the boat, to question the *status quo*. It actually nibbles at the delicate edges of our fragile independence and dupes us into retaining a number of symbolic trappings such as the Monarchy, the

Governor General and the Privy Council, long after their usefulness had disappeared. Still, whether sooner or later, abandoning these trappings is best handled with delicacy regardless of how we may feel about them. We should not make enemies unnecessarily, especially during the earliest days of our journey as a fledgling nation. The sentiment does have residual value even at this late stage in the pursuit of long overdue transformation.

To think that we may transform the nature of traditional Democracy or rearrange its priorities by engaging systems and processes that are its mirror image is delusional. We must begin at the point of need of our people, not at the point of assumption that traditional Democracy will effectively address any and all of these needs. This illogic is where we went astray in the very first place. Somehow our oppressors convinced us that it is a better arrangement to place the cart ahead of the horse and not the other way around. Unlike us, they did not lose sight of their own best interests. We should not forget that at the outset we were not people but chattel imbued only with the value that our owners unilaterally assessed. Of course, this was based strictly on inhumane capitalist economic dogma. If we understand this, we will surely come to realize that there is nothing to be gained from continually hoping that traditional two-party-system-democracy will eventually solve our intractable problems. Our rescue lies in an apolitical approach that recognizes the stark deficiencies of the flawed system we inherited and continue to embrace addictively; now, perhaps, with some confusion and faint embarrassment.

Many will say that it is simply wishful to think that we can, in fact, approach what are essentially political problems in an apolitical fashion. This is not unexpected. Upon reflection we will come to realize soon enough that this is a specious argument whose origin resides firmly within the maelstrom that is traditional Democracy. If we can ever genuinely come to put our people and their needs first, there is no doubt that we can slay or so maim the chimera of destructive, adversarial politics that politics as we now know it would cease to hold sway over our lives. This is what is meant by an apolitical approach: people and country first. This is impossible with politics as it is in Jamaica. Political party and party politics would have no place in this transformed landscape. There is no doubt that a government of national unity would provide the best opportunity to achieve the transformation we seek and desperately need.

Put in perspective, what is required here is a change in mindset that is at least equal to that which must have taken place when the British government and many among our former slave masters came to realize the general worthlessness of slavery and abandoned the principle of enslavement in favor of a system that allowed some semblance of personal freedom among the formerly enslaved. As we may all imagine, few at the time thought this change possible, and for good reason. We have therefore come to understand and appreciate the fact that in human relationships what is possible can always be made to happen. Changing our blinkered view of traditional Democracy is clearly possible. I have changed my own view with what I consider considerable justification. So can you. There is nothing to prevent this but you. This is true for us as individuals no less than it is true for those who constitute the leadership class. Conviction and will are the most crucial prerequisites. The surest way to prevent this transformation nationally is to continue to hold fast to the irrationality that traditional Democracy and only traditional Democracy can lead us and others like us out of our proverbial wilderness into a symbolic Promised Land.

We cannot continue to insist that two-party-system-democracy is of superior value to the welfare of our people and the best interests of the nation. Such ridiculous conceit clearly places the means of getting to virtuous government ahead of the end purpose of virtuous government which has to be the greatest good for the greatest number of citizens. While the end cannot always justify the means, the end is surely always superior as a value to any means applied toward its realization. As survivors of slavery and the descendants of slaves, it is sickening that we have become so indifferent to the clearly outrageous reversal of this paradigm in the name of traditional Democracy. The extent to which we remain committed to its questionable claims is frightening. The primary requirement for steady, reliable focus on the people and their welfare does not require traditional Democracy since this strain of Democracy is but one means to this end. Instead, the most primary of requirements in this regard has to be unwavering commitment to the welfare of the people along with action that clearly validates and supports this commitment. Two-party-system-democracy in Jamaica cannot legitimately claim to have ever met, or to currently meet, this essential requirement.

As we have seen, there are competitive systems that do meet this requirement to an extent that is measurably greater than traditional Democracy does. Given the history of poor performance and dubious accomplishments under two-party-system-democracy in Jamaica and comparable former colonies, there is every reason to conclude that this system is unlikely to address our problems effectively. Continued unquestioning reliance on this system is therefore unwarranted. The time has come for a new approach. Such an approach is what is being proposed here.

I am aware that there is at least one small group of middle class Jamaicans that recently initiated an house-hopping campaign going from house to house in suburbia, intent on building support for a third political party. This has been attempted before with less than marginal success and is likely to fare even worse now. I cannot envisage such an effort achieving any degree of meaningful, competitive functionality. In light of what we have come to understand of the two-party-system-democracy it should be obvious that adding to the number of political parties has but a single likely outcome: increasing the already excessively high levels of dysfunction in politics and in the leadership class and further splintering the electorate. The evidence appears to indicate that such an eventuality would only serve to increase the already scalding temperature of corrupt, destructive, adversarial politics.

There is no justification for continuing to ignore or misread signs that clearly indicate the need for a change in direction. Even if we believe that the alternative being proposed is implausible, we can certainly agree that a change in direction is imperative. The frightening reality is that change is, in fact, occurring even as we contemplate and discuss our dilemma and any steps we may take to address it. The much more frightening reality, however, is the fact that this change is occurring by default with the inevitability of air rushing in to fill a vacuum but without our purposeful input, guidance, management or leadership. To those who would instinctively reject what is being proposed the challenge is simply this: what would you propose as a more viable, promising alternative? Not only is the *status quo* not an alternative, it is utterly unsustainable.

b.   The Big Picture & the Big Four

The big picture has to be framed by our national vision as defined in **Vision 2030 Jamaica**: *"Jamaica, the place of choice to live, work, raise families and do business"*. To lose sight of this is to guarantee that we will lose our way once again. This does require an extended span of attention individually as well as collectively. Regrettably, our attention span has also fallen victim to the painful battering of our dire circumstances. Yet, we must find a way to look beyond our constant discomfort and pain in order to allow ourselves the very best opportunity to embrace our vision with unceasing awareness to the point of permanence so that its exercise is as natural as our infectious laughter. None can deny the challenge that this presents since we have already observed the powerful, coercive influence of our circumstances over our ability to maintain constant focus even on our needs.

The primary responsibility to maintain focus on our vision has to rest with our leaders and, most significantly, with our Prime Minister. The maximum leader must be the keeper and preacher of our vision. This person has no higher professional obligation than this because this, after all, is our personal and collective purpose. Every act of our leaders has to reflect alignment with and commitment to our vision. The Prime Minister must therefore place the identified core priorities of crime, agriculture, tourism and education (CATE) at the center of his focus in the pursuit of living our vision. To fall short on this account is to entice failure.

Understanding the impact of acting on CATE as the core priority is to understand its broad, dramatic multiplier effect on our individual and general national welfare. In addition, this more than anything else enhances our ability to capitalize on opportunities now invisible to us because of our self-inflicted myopia. Imagine meeting our 2030 target of reducing major crime to 43/100,000 people in ten years, doubling the number of returning nationals in five, achieving full employment in ten, growth in our tourist industry in excess of 5% per year in three, and reducing our national debt to less than 100% of GDP in twelve! Impossible? Not at all, in my humble opinion. As an added incentive to advancing conviction and will, I challenge the econometricians and sociologists among us to do the calculations and tell us in dollars and cultural impact what all of this would mean. No doubt the resulting values would enhance our desire, comprehension and will to accomplish the tasks that would lead to the realization of these possibilities. Just imagine the extent of the transformation that would come to pass!

There is little reason to doubt our potential or opportunity quotient (OQ, i.e. the ratio of the proportion of opportunity realized to the overall extent of available, acknowledged opportunity). There is even less rationality in downgrading the possibilities to be exploited. The big picture requires us to be bold and courageous, not doubtful and faint-hearted. For nations, as for individuals, the future is always there but we may effectively reach for it only if we have a vision of what we expect to become. Regrettably, we face the intrinsic danger of being excessively tribal, timid and shortsighted, given our history since Independence. Among the most profound examples of this is the all but palpable fact that we appear unable to see our future free of the demeaning scourge of garrisons and crime as well as politicians constantly more committed to party and self than to country. We must come to realize that this is a choice we have made to accept things as they are. It is distinctly possible to choose differently. The mechanics and processes proposed here in regard to governance and national priorities should engender greater willingness to review a number of the choices that we have made, starting from the earliest years of our Independence, with the intention of abandoning some, advancing others and making new and more confidently transformative ones. It cannot be said too often: the *status quo* is as obstructive as it is untenable.

To parody the Billy Joel song about the city of New York, we must now put ourselves in a truly Jamaica state of mind by envisioning our future differently and in colour. We alone hold our future in our hands and hearts; we alone can fix what ails us. We must believe. We must act. While the focus of visible, national leadership responsibility will always reside in our maximum leader, by convention for executive purposes, we the people must surely understand our role in keeping the big picture in focus at all times. It is interesting to observe that while we may have lost our ability or willingness to focus on our needs for extended periods, this has never ever been true of our focus on political party affiliation. The commitment and energy we unwaveringly apply to this tribally infused occupation must be redirected to the more useful and inclusive purpose of national unity and nation building.

Among all NGO entities in the country, the one with the greatest potential to facilitate a national redirection of focus has to be the church. I am not a religious person, but I am not indifferent to the significant and historic role of the church and religion in our country. The church as an institution should mend its many fractures in deference to the indisputable need for unity in our nation and become a beacon for what is possible when religious unity and noble purpose are aligned.

The congruence of religion and politics does mean that the difficulty of the church arriving at functional unity is every bit as challenging as is the case for our two political parties. However, given the church's far more exemplary and steadfast commitment to people and their welfare, movement by the church toward functional unity is likely to be achieved earlier than is likely in the political arena. This may be exactly the catalyst that is needed. Politicians in both parties, along with many of their die-hard followers, can be expected to rail against this suggested initiative by the church. Should conflict ensue the church has the advantage, I believe, since the church will be far more able to enlist the support of other influential NGOs in this most worthy cause. In addition, our politicians are indeed running out of options to mislead as their credibility continues to decline. Given the historically low voter turnout at the last parliamentary elections, it appears that they may also be running out of the number of people predisposed to being misled.

11

NEXT STEPS

It is not unusual that there is a silver lining behind most dark clouds. In this sense we may be fortunate. Behind the ominous dark clouds of our national dilemma is this not so insignificant realization: we all know and acknowledge the primary drivers of our looming disaster. They deserve repetition at every opportunity: crime and corruption, political polarization, chronic unemployment especially among the youth, inadequate opportunity for outstanding early childhood education, maddening addiction to the *status quo* and reluctance or unwillingness to address our problems with conviction and will. This means that we do not need to re-invent the wheel by engaging consultants or experts at distressing expense to determine what is wrong. Neither do we need these experts to tell us what needs to be done in response.

In fact, triage is already complete. The patient is moribund, the operating theatre is prepared and the surgeons are gowned and gloved with scalpels at the ready to perform the delicate, highly invasive surgery. We need not worry about the recovery room since this is where the patient has been residing for an inordinate amount of time in limbo, not knowing which of two options is to be exercised: discharge or return to the operating room. We are now certain that discharge is altogether out of the question. Notwithstanding the natural fear of the surgery, it has to be done. We must now begin to consciously act on this account to ensure that we not merely manage the procedure but ensure the best possible outcome. These are the most critical things that national leadership must initiate immediately in concert with the people:

1. Reach agreement on CATE as the core priorities to be addressed immediately along with the overall process to be engaged in their address.

2. Market the ideas of the proposed fundamental change with the fervor, intent and real time measurement of effectiveness common among world class, successful commercial enterprises such as our own GraceKennedy. The apolitical nature of this effort cannot be overemphasized.

3. Declare war on the *status quo* with the conviction and purpose of the leadership of a country that is under siege (which we are, in fact).

4. Really sell **Vision 2030 Jamaica** as a salvation document and plan that offers the greatest promise of arresting our decline and stimulating measurable recovery and long-term growth.

5. Relentlessly identify and focus on points of accountability with the emphasis and intensity of the leadership typical of the most successful of world class commercial enterprises.

6. Quantify and isolate the budget for **Vision 2030 Jamaica** under the office of the Prime Minister. The maximum leader must accept maximum responsibility and accountability and must be seen to do so.

7. Implement the identified priority projects with the active engagement and involvement of all citizens, individually and collectively at all levels of influential private, public, social and commercial interface.

8. Measure performance & outcomes with a passion born of the will to succeed and give credit lavishly to responsible agents and agencies when goals are met.

9. Evaluate overall progress against priorities within the overall **Vision 2030 Jamaica** plan with budgets, timelines & justified adjustments as backdrops.

10. Ceaselessly obtain & show respect for feedback from the people by engaging in regular community meetings to communicate progress and anticipated or actual adjustments to process and activity against every priority project.

Happily, a reading of the **Vision 2030 Jamaica** document will reveal that a number of these steps is clearly stated there. This does mean that others are not merely aware of our dilemma but have thought about it and have taken steps in the address of it. Not surprisingly, **Vision 2030 Jamaica** does not and should not be expected to address the fundamental issue of national governance. However, this limitation in no way diminishes either the timeliness or potency of the Plan. It presents us with opportunity, structure and direction. We surely cannot allow **Vision 2030 Jamaica** to become simply a point of reference for exemplary, elegant planning and a lasting example of unaddressed possibilities.

FINAL WORDS

At the outset, I was unaware of **Vision 2030 Jamaica**. I consider it a most favorable if fortuitous coincidence to have come across this impressively elegant national plan at the time I did. The Plan has not only made the task at hand easier and simpler; it brings remarkable perspective, balance and structure in a distinctly practical manner to the sense of need and urgency that I envisage as vital in the address of Jamaica's ongoing dilemma. The Plan also confirms the conviction that while Jamaica may indeed be resource challenged in a number of respects, there can be no doubt that were we able to harness and effectively manage our scarce resources, especially in respect of manpower, we could overcome our critical challenges with impressive speed and exemplary success. It may be, after all, that the main reason we appear to be so resource deficient as a country has much less to do with the perceived shortage of resources and much more to do with our inability to utilize the available resources effectively.

The remarkably disproportionate, jealousy-triggering rate of individual and collective success among the Jamaica Diaspora clearly supports the latter point of view. It is less the amount of resources than how these resources are employed that is the problem. This reality makes it very difficult to imagine just where the cap may be for the quite discernible OQ that this equation reveals. Leadership, management, conviction and will, account for the major causal gap in the equation. One has to admit that, as a nation, we do appear to enjoy a rather disproportionately high OQ. This is not merely energizing but bolsters the conviction that we are in the enviable position of being more likely than not to overcome our intractable problems. We need to modify the traditional and current instruments of governance or create new ones with clearly recognizable potential for transforming our political landscape. If there are former slave colonies that may reasonably be seen as capable of arresting seemingly endless decline and most likely to initiate a growth surge, Jamaica would have to be considered most favorably among these. Our success or failure resides with us.

Undoubtedly, there are several approaches that may be taken to address Jamaica's dilemma. These include violent rebellion against the *status quo*, the use of the ballot box to dump political moochers and non-performers, the rise of a dictator class perhaps from the security forces (the army or constabulary or both), the wholesale usurpation of the major functions of local and national government by the class of dons. The first has historical roots but in today's world is unlikely to be successful or sustainable; the second has never been tried and is all but impossible to contemplate; the third is the most unlikely of all given the history and capability of the institutions involved; the last is actually a work in progress on a micro-scale and, sadly, has a better than even chance of success if left to consolidate its currently dispersed power and influence. Some believe that there are two additional approaches: hope and prayer. Unfortunately, neither is viable as both are passive approaches without the potential to generate transformative action. In addition, both more or less effectively support the *status quo* by virtue of their religious inclination and historical tendency to await a savior for deliverance. In addition, there is no doubt that these approaches have always been and continue to be applied with no evidence of positive effect.

Regrettably, we have come to demand and expect less, rather than more, of ourselves and our leaders. We are so battered and bruised by our terrible communal and national circumstances that vast numbers of us no longer look or see beyond the duration of our pain which, understandably, we try to assuage as speedily as we can. We have become indifferent to our possibilities and potential. As a result, we have come to confine ourselves to an imagination space that is no more than days, weeks or months. We appear to have concluded that commitment to long-term considerations is an unaffordable luxury. This explains in part our traditional indifference to all the extended national plans with which we have been presented. We must view and treat **Vision 2030 Jamaica** differently if for no other reason than that it does offer much more opportunity for escape from the *status quo* than any other national plan since Independence.

Under the weight of history which demonstrates that satisfaction of needs is increasingly an unlikely prospect, our needs generally degrade to distant wishes and time has no meaningful duration beyond that of our pain. We do not, nor are we willing to, imagine ourselves beyond the immediate. This is what being trapped in a state of perpetual uncertainty caused by what now appears to be interminable crime, corruption, high unemployment, poverty and political malfeasance does to a people. Most disconcerting of all, this entrapment interferes in profound ways with our vision of ourselves. In short, it disassembles and obscures our future. The question then becomes: how can we envision ourselves in a future so muddled we wonder if it exists at all? Ultimately we are more confined by our very restricted imagination than by the threshold of our pain. It is therefore crucial that we escape the incapacitating effects imposed by our dysfunctional environment. Essentially, this entire work is an attempt to do just this.

We have examined the trajectory of our distant, recent and current history in an attempt to explain the irony and contradictions inherent in the two-party-system-democracy that we have long accepted without question. We have emphasized the overarching responsibility and accountability of government more definitively. At the same time, we have proposed a dramatic if not revolutionary change in the mechanics and processes of governance while expanding the explicit involvement, responsibility and accountability of the general leadership class, NGOs and the ordinary citizen. Nevertheless, I quite understand the frequently unfavorable or even hostile response to many of the ideas proposed in this work. With or without discernible acquiescence or open acceptance, the more thoughtful reader may no doubt come to understand why I just as frequently reject such responses. Our circumstances demand that we invoke a cycle of contrarian thinking or outright rejection of the *status quo* in order that we may effectively escape its progress-denying gravity.

In any event, there can be no disagreement that our circumstances are dire. Neither can anyone dispute the need to act preemptively to secure and protect our nation's future. This is what directs my steadfast refusal to be detained or held hostage by our history or be constrained by our ambushed, captive national imagination. I have dared to be disruptively imaginative and bold in my contribution to the ongoing debate about the state of affairs in our country. It is in this spirit that I ask my fellow citizens to approach this effort in a manner that is fully respectful of the historic nature of our challenges and the sacred obligation we should all feel toward the future of our children as well as to the future of the generations to follow. It is time that we cease being a work in progress to become a work of progress.

There has never been a time when Bob Marley's exhortation to free ourselves from mental slavery was as instructive as it is now. There can be no doubt whatsoever that we are free from physical bondage and have been for some time. What is equally clear is that our national psyche has never fully distanced itself from mirroring the outlook of our former oppressors or their surrogates. As a consequence, we find enormous security in the *status quo* and are consistently afraid of change. In fact, the more a courageous few among us attempt to redirect our outlook, the more ferociously we tend to reject such attempts and to extol the claimed virtues of the *status quo*.

While our national pace of positive change has slowed to less than a crawl since 1962, the reality is that we have in fact been working at change even before then. Many have already accepted this stagnation as the way things have to be. Their resignation is embedded in the *status quo*. Naturally, this makes them a part of the dilemma we face. Yet, resignation does not have to be a permanent state. Consider what Canada has been able to accomplish in its fight against being fractured by what was once seen as an insurmountable language problem. The story is made more meaningful when we see that a Jamaican was actively engaged in the achievement of Canada's success in addressing this unquestionably monumental problem.

In the **Ottawa Citizen ePaper** of June 17, 2013, Keith Spicer reveals the innovative, politically sensitive, community-co-opting manner in which Canada effectively addressed its nationally divisive language problem over a period of 50 years. Spicer provides a great lesson in how best to approach such a potentially explosive national issue. It should be noted that Spicer was the first Commissioner of Official Languages under the Canadian Official Languages Act of 1969. In his revelation, *How Canada met its bilingualism challenge*, Spicer acknowledges the pivotal role played by Jamaican Lloyd Stanford in the realization of successful outcomes under the Act. The nationally disruptive potential of the language problem in Canada was always readily acknowledged internationally. The problem was exacerbated by the very controversial francophone exhortation, *Vive le Québec libre* (Long live free Québec), of Former French President Charles de Gaulle, during a public address in Montreal in 1967.

The fact that the problem has been overcome is remarkable. Clearly, the very difficult is not necessarily improbable. It is a relevant and not too distant an exemplary lesson from which Jamaica and its political class could benefit greatly.

The time has come to pay more attention and assign greater credibility to alternatives or options in the manner in which we confront our problems. As a people we must come to understand that we create tradition. Tradition does not and should not overwhelmingly determine who we are or how we address our intractable problems. In the final analysis, tradition is our servant not our master.

REFERENCES

Alexander, Michelle, *The New Jim Crow: Mass Incarceration in the Age of Colourblindness*

Best of SkyWritings, The, Linda Gambrill, editor, Air Jamaica's Inflight Magazine, September 1972 - August 2002, *A Tapestry of Jamaica*

Blake, Duane, *Shower Posse*

Carson, Ben, M.D. with Candy Carson, *America the Beautiful*

Clarke, Edith, *My Mother Who Fathered Me: A Study of the Family in Three Selected Communities of Jamaica*

Fanon, Frantz, *Studies In A Dying Colonialism*

Gray, Obika, *Demeaned but Empowered, The Social Power of the Urban Poor in Jamaica*

Grindley, Gerry, *Judas Mentality*

Gunst, Laurie, *Born Fi Dead: A Journey Through The Jamaican Posse Underworld*

James, C.L.R., *The Black Jacobins*

James, Owen Everard, *Brackets. A Book of Poems...*

James, Owen Everard, *Jamaican by Birth American by Choice*

Kupchan, Charles A., *No One's World: The West, the Rising Rest, and the Coming Global Turn*,

Manley, Michael, *The Politics of Change: A Jamaican Testament*

Manley, Rachel, *Drumblair: Memories of a Jamaican Childhood*

Nettleford, Rex M., *Caribbean Cultural Identity: The case of Jamaica*

Planning Institute of Jamaica, The, *Vision 2030 Jamaica National Development Plan (Popular Version)*

Roth, David, *Sacred Honor, A Biography: Colin Powell, The Inside Account Of His Life And Triumphs*

Seaga, Edward, *My Life And Leadership, Volume 1: Clash of Ideologies 1930 - 1980*

Senior, Olive, *A - Z of Jamaica Heritage*

Sherlock, Philip M. & Hazel Bennett, *The Story of the Jamaican People*

Smith-Chang, Dr. Mildred, *The Mask is Off*

Stolzoff, Norman C., *Wake the Town & Tell the People: Dancehall Culture in Jamaica*

Thomson, Ian, *The Dead Yard (A Story of Modern Jamaica)*

Tutu, Desmond, *No Future Without Forgiveness*

Walters, Ewart, *To Follow Right....A journalist's journey*

Williams, Eric, *Capitalism and Slavery*

Articles, Papers, Digital

Bank of Jamaica, External Sector Statistics Unit, *The Balance Of Payments, Remittance Update, March 2010*

Bertram, Arnold (Contributor), The Gleaner, June 4, 2006, *The 1938 riots (Part II): The urban masses follow*

Bertram, Arnold (Contributor), The Gleaner, May 28, 2006, *The 1938 Frome labour riots (Part I)*

Blackman, Sir Courtney, Ph.D., Caribbean Corporate Leadership Conference, Barbados, November 12-13, 2007, *Management, Economic Development And Caribbean Corporate Leadership*

Bolland, Nigel, *On the March: Labor Rebellions in the British Caribbean, 1934-39*, Ian Randle Publishers, Kingston, Jamaica

Boyne, Ian, (Contributor), The Sunday Gleaner, July 29, 2012, *Eddie Seaga: Born Jamaican*

Chandrasekaran, Maya, *The 1938 Labor Revolt-An Uprising of Ideas and Words*

Chang, Kevin O'Brien, The Gleaner, June 13, 2010, *The Road To A Cruel Jamaica*

Donella Meadows Archive, The, *Singapore Leads the Good Life Under a Benevolent Dictator*

Forbes, Marcia, Ph.D., March 12, 2012, Caribbean Journal, *Women in Jamaica*

Garvey, Marcus, [Internet]. 2013. The Biography Channel website. Available from http://www.biography.com/people/marcus-garvey-9307319 [Accessed 04 Jun 2013]

Gleaner Newspaper Archives, *Pieces of the Past, A New Era in Jamaica's History: The Founding of the People's National Party*

Gleaner, The, January 14, 2013, *Gov't Not Ready - Former PNP State Minister Accuses Administration Of Ineffective Management*

Gleaner, The, June 12, 2011, *Jamaican Diaspora A Key Partner For Economic Growth*

Gleaner, The, September 9, 2010, *Jamaican Scientist To Give Int'l Address On Local Medicinal Research*

Glennie, Alex and Laura Chapell, Institute for Public Policy Research, June 2010, Country Profiles, *Jamaica: From Diverse Beginning to Diaspora in the Developed World*

Hart, Richard, Caribbean Labour Solidarity and Socialist History Society, 2002, *Labour Relations of the 1930s in the British Caribbean Region Colonies*

Henry, Martin, Contributor, August 5, 2012, The Gleaner, *Jamaica 50: Achievements, Failures, Setbacks*

http://www.biography.com/people/*lee-kuan-yew*-9377339 [Accessed 12 Jan 2013]

h t t p : / / w w w . f o x n e w s . c o m / w o r l d / 2 0 1 2 / 0 4 / 1 7 / *jamaican-lottery-scams-spread-despite-us-crackdown*/#ixzz2NdmaQ9X0

James, Owen Everard, (Contributor) Caribbean American Passport, March 2013, *Jamaica: The Epicenter of Crisis in the Caribbean*

Kingstone, Steve, BBC News Latin America & Caribbean, 27 May 2010, *Scared and hungry in Jamaica's Tivoli Gardens*

Lindsay, Louis, (A New Introduction) *The Myth of Independence: Middle Class Politics and Non-Mobilization in Jamaica*

Luton, Daraine, Senior Staff Reporter, The Gleaner, June 17, 2013, *Diaspora Conferences - WASTED!*

Meditz, Sandra W. and Dennis M. Hanratty, editors, *Caribbean Islands: A Country Study*

Morgan, Henley, The Observer, October 03, 2012, *Our men are killing us*

Padmore, George (editor), 1945, *The Voice of Coloured Labour*

Persaud, Wilberne (Columnist), The Gleaner, January 8, 2010, Commentary - *Comparing Singapore to Jamaica*

Poverty Reduction and Economic Management Unit, Caribbean Countries Management Unit Latin America and the Caribbean Region, Report No. 60374-JM, *Jamaica Country Economic Memorandum, Unlocking Growth*

Quill, Dennie, (Contributor) The Gleaner, November 9, 2007, *Corruption in Jamaica: Sloppy administration or malfeasance?*

Spicer, Keith, *How Canada met its bilingualism challenge*, Ottawa Citizen ePaper, Monday, June 17, 2013

Schwartz, Mattathias, The New Yorker, December 12, 2011, *A Massacre in Jamaica (After the United States demanded the extradition of a drug lord, a bloodletting ensued.)*

Thame, Maziki, University of the West Indies, Mona, Jamaica, *Reading Violence and Postcolonial Decolonization through Fanon: The Case of Jamaica*

Thomas-Hope, Elizabeth, The United Nations Population Fund through The Planning Office of Jamaica, 2004, *Migration Situation Analysis, Policy And Programme Needs For Jamaica*

Transatlantic Academy, *The Democratic Disconnect, Citizenship and Accountability in the Transatlantic Community*

Wedderburn, Chantel, Eric P. Chiang, Rupert Rhodd, Journal of International Business and Cultural Studies, *The Informal Economy in Jamaica: Is it feasible to tax this sector?*

Wignall, Mark, Jamaica Observer, June 17, 2012, *Who first gave them guns?*

Wignall, Mark, Jamaica Observer, May 30, 2010, *Something-went-horribly-wrong-in-Tivoli-Gardens*

Will, George F., The Washington Post, Opinions, January 2, 2013, *Our Decadent Democracy*

www.caribbean360.com/http://www.caribbean360.com/index.php/news/jamaicanews/655835.html**,** *Doctors condemn execution-style murder at Jamaica hospital*

Ying, Neville, Professor, Melesha Manderson, Aika Smith, Jamaica Diaspora Foundation/Jamaica Diaspora Institute, July 2010, *Jamaica Diaspora Governance and Operational Structure: The Way Forward*